Well Done!

A 30-day Journey into Financial Discipleship.

"Well done, good and faithful servant. You have been faithful over a little; I will set you over much. Enter into the joy of your master."   (Matthew 25:21,22)

By Peter J. Briscoe

Well Done!

Bible references

Verses identified as (ESV) are taken from The ESV® Bible (The Holy Bible, English Standard Version®). ESV® Text Edition: 2016. Copyright © 2001 by Cross-way, a publishing ministry of Good News Publishers. The ESV® text has been reproduced in cooperation with and by permission of Good News Publishers. Unauthorized reproduction of this publication is prohibited. All rights reserved.

Verses identified as (NLT) are taken from the Holy Bible, New Living Translation, copyright © 1996, 2004, 2015 by Tyndale House Foundation. Used by permission of Tyndale House Publishers, Inc., Carol Stream, Illinois 60188. All rights reserved. Verses identified as (TLB) are taken from The Living Bible, copyright © 1971 by Tyndale House Foundation. Used by permission of Tyndale House Publishers Inc., Carol Stream, Illinois 60188. All rights reserved.

Verses identified as (NKJV) are taken from the New King James Version®. Copyright © 1982 by Thomas Nelson. Used by permission. All rights reserved. Verses identified as (CEV) are taken from the Contemporary English Version®, Copyright © 1995 American Bible Society. All rights reserved.

Verses identified as (RSV) are taken from the Revised Standard Version of the Bible, copyright ©1946, 1952, and 1971 the Division of Christian Education of the National Council of the Churches of Christ in the United States of America. Used by permission. All rights reserved. All other verses are taken from THE HOLY BIBLE, NEW INTERNATIONAL VERSION®, NIV®
Copyright © 1973, 1978, 1984, 2011 by Biblica, Inc.® Used by permission. All rights reserved worldwide.

Well Done, by Peter J. Briscoe
Copyright Peter J. Briscoe
ISBN: 978-90-832285-0-1
February 2022
All rights reserved
Published by Compass – finances God's way, European office
www.compass1.eu
info@compass1.eu

To learn more about Compass in Europe,
visit www. compass1.eu

Contents

Foreword

" Well done, good and faithful servant. You have been faithful over a little; I will set you over much. Enter into the joy of your master." Wow! Can you imagine hearing this one day from Jesus?

As humans, we crave positive feedback. It feeds our soul, affirms our identity, and communicates that we're doing a good job. Whether
it comes from our family, friends, boss, or colleagues, praise and approval reinforce the value of our efforts.

Getting a "good job" or an "I'm proud of you" hits the mark and has us feeling good for the day, sometimes even for the week. Hearing *"Well done!"* from Jesus Christ Himself, on the other hand, will elicit an entirely different response – one that includes pure worship, joy, exhilaration, unrestrained singing and dancing in the streets, gratefulness, and praise. It will be the stuff of eternity, with Jesus rewarding a life lived for Him.

So then, what really matters to Jesus, and how do we know we're on the right track?

In his latest book in the Financial Discipleship series, Peter explores this question and more. Organized as a four-part, 30-day devotional, the driving force behind Well Done is this: Jesus calls us to multiply.

Well Done, when we apply its content and later hear the words for ourselves, will be profound. These two words will set the course for the rest of our eternity. For Christians, this is our end goal and what fuels how we live today. It's why we embrace the Good News, surrender our lives to Jesus, commit to serving Him and others, and do our best to glorify God every day through our

thoughts and actions. It's our ultimate positive feedback and eternal reward for going all in for Christ here on earth.

Thank you for investing in your eternal future. Before you embark on this devotional journey, I encourage you to read the full parable of the talent passages found in Matthew 25:14-30 and Luke 19:11-27. Pray for insight and wisdom, read slowly, and ask yourself two fundamental questions: Why was the master pleased? What does it mean for me?

Enjoy the book and let us know if we can help you on your financial discipleship journey. Praise God for your desire to live for Jesus and embrace financial discipleship as a core component to following Him fully. You are well on your way to hearing *"Well done!"* the day you meet Jesus.

Brandon Sieben, CEO, Compass – finances God's way

About the Author

Peter Briscoe, born in 1950 in the UK, and studied Industrial Chemistry and Management at Loughborough University of Technology. He moved to The Netherlands in 1974 and was asked by his company to set up a subsidiary in Holland, selling chemical specialties to the aerospace and food processing industries. From 1986 to 1990, Peter was Executive Director of CBMC, Christian Businessmen's Committees, in Holland. CBMC is dedicated to making disciples amongst business and professional people.

In 1990, Peter set up "Synthesys, a consulting company in chemical product development. When the Berlin Wall collapsed in 1990, Peter developed Europartners, a movement dedicated to reaching and discipling European business and professional leaders for Christ.
From 2002, Peter took an assignment as Managing Director of HE Space Operations, serving the European Space institutions, specializing in providing professional services for spaceflight activities.

From 2020, Peter retired from active business to develop a movement of financial discipleship in Europe, which is now active in over 20 nations.
He is married to his Dutch wife, Didie since 1972. They are blessed with three daughters and six grandchildren.

Day 1: Introduction

I have been a Christian for around 55 years and have had a business career spanning over 45. I have been married to a wonderful wife for 50 years and am a father of three married daughters and a grandfather of six great kids. I have started three businesses and employed quite a few people. I have started the European Economic Forum, Britain's National Prayer Breakfast, and the International Association for the Advancement of Space Safety. I pioneered two international Christian movements, two local ones, and served two terms of six years each as chair of our church board. I could mention more.

However, I would like to state with Paul, "But whatever gain I had, I counted as loss for the sake of Christ. Indeed, I count everything as loss because of the surpassing worth of knowing Christ Jesus my Lord" (Philippians 3:7-8).
In my journey of financial discipleship, I have made multiple mistakes and done some things that I am ashamed to remember. I often have feelings of inadequacy and shortcoming. I feel as though I could have done so much more, so much better.

The beautiful part of it all is that God still loves me. He loved me the same amount in the good times and in the not so good times; He never stopped pursuing me, and I never gave up on Him. He never turned His back on me. He had every right to not want anything to do with me. However, He is always right there with a big smile and arms wide-open.
If there is one thing Jesus said that has been a guiding light for all I have done in life, it would be what He said to His faithful servants in Matthew 25. "Well done, good and faithful servant.
Enter into the joy of your master."
I long to hear Jesus say those words to me.

Well Done!

Jesus told a parable in which two faithful servants were given large sums of money to work with and provide a return on the master's investment. When the master returned from a long absence, he rewarded these two faithful servants and said to them both, "*Well done, good and faithful servant. You have been faithful over a little; I will set you over much. Enter into the joy of your master*" (Matthew 25:21, 23).
Every Christian longs to hear these words from Jesus' lips in heaven. The question that logically follows is, What should I be doing now to someday hear these words and enter into the joy of our Master?

First, I have to recognize my ability. In the parable, each servant's amount to invest matched his ability. Faithful servants take whatever they have and use it to the best of their ability.
It's not about how much ability you have: it's what do you do with it. Both servants got the same reward because they did what they could with what they had been given. I am certainly not the most gifted speaker, the most efficient manager, the most inspiring leader, the most creative product developer, the most interesting writer, the most loving husband and father. I just want to do the best with what I have and am, be it ever so limited.

Then, I have to recognize my responsibility to use the opportunities God gives me to multiply the resources He entrusts to me. Some of us will have bigger circles of influence or larger bags of gold, but we are all given the same responsibility. We are made to multiply. The most basic form of multiplication is to bear children. Not all are physically capable of bearing children, and some choose not to. That's okay. However, we are all called to multiply spiritually, to invest our lives in others to help them become disciples and to grow in the faith. We can multiply what we have been given, our ideas and thoughts to serve and love people.

Last, I have to recognize my accountability. In our story, the master left for a while and then came back. Jesus is going to come back,

and one day I will have to give an account. The question will be, What did you do with what I gave you?
One manager in the parable quoted above was held accountable for being fearful and doing nothing beneficial with the resources given to him. The other two managers were praised for doing good and being faithful. These two qualities are what the Master is looking for. Faithfulness is doing what God asks us to do: to conduct our life and work according to His ways so that He can rely on us to do what He wants and carry out His instructions.

Part One will help us to "begin with the end in mind." The better our perspective on what will be happening in the future, the better our decisions will be today. If I, as a businessman, know that the market for my products will be huge in three years, I know how to invest today to get ready for that harvest! Jesus is returning to gather His people. I am going to heaven to
spend an eternity with Him. That's a fact. When? I have no idea. People have asked me frequently, "Do you see signs of Jesus' imminent return?" I always respond, "I don't know. But when I look in the mirror, I see a lot of signs that I will soon be going! One way or another, I will be with the Lord soon!" Part One is all about seeing our eternal destiny and getting prepared.

Part Two builds on the necessity of preparing to meet Jesus. He does not want to build institutions or programs, although these can be useful. His goal is to build people. I believe that the fruit of the Spirit is what the Lord wants to multiply in us, building our character to be people He can use for His
purposes. I remember one of my mentors in business saying, "Remember, customers do not pay you for what you know, how well educated or intelligent or skillful you are, or even how excellent your product is. They pay you for being useful in helping them meet their goals." In some way, I believe
this to be the same for Christians. We will be praised, not for being knowledgeable or what we have achieved, but for being useful to the Lord to accomplish His purposes. The contribution of our life is what counts.

Well Done!

Part Three will discuss ways in which we can practically organize our financial resources to optimize their use for the Lord's purposes. The three servants in our parable were given huge sums of money to do business with. A talent was the equivalent of approximately sixteen years of average income! If we will be held accountable to Jesus for what we have done with the money He has entrusted to us, how should we manage our income and expenses? What is the purpose of building wealth? One of the most important questions to ask ourselves is, How much is enough? Enough for what? Can we multiply the resources we have been given for the Master's use just as the two servants in our parable did?

Part Four will look at financial discipleship and how we can help others to become financial disciples. The most precious resources we have been given are our relationships with others. If we begin with the end in mind, the question we have to ask is, Who will be with us in eternity? When I became a Christian at age 16, I remember the youth rally speaker saying,
"If you were the only person alive, Christ would still have died for you!"
He gave His life so that many might live. This is the prize – to help others hear, *"Well done, good and faithful servant. Enter into the joy of your master!"*

This book is all about making your financial discipleship decisions in the light of eternity. Some immortal words by Robert Frost in his poem "The Road Not Taken" describe the importance of making the right choices.
> "Two roads diverged in a wood,
> and I, I chose the one less traveled by.
> And that has made all the difference."

Frost was teasing a friend who always blamed his life circumstances on some random past decision, looking back and saying the other path would have been better. I do hope that, at the end of our days, we can look back without regret at the choices we made.

Living in the light of eternity will make us more effective and fruitful for Christ in this world. I love this quote from C.S. Lewis from his book *Mere Christianity:* "If you read history, you will find that the Christians who did most for the present world were just those who thought most of the next… It is since Christians have largely ceased to think of the other world that they have become so ineffective in this. Aim at Heaven and you will get earth "thrown in": aim at earth and you will get neither."
I hope you will choose the road less traveled!

This book is not an easy read for a quiet Sunday afternoon. It is meant to be read in bite-sized pieces, to be chewed over and meditated on.
It contains reading for a 30-day devotional period. A day's reading takes about 20 minutes. I would encourage you to read a chapter a day, then stop and ask the Lord what he would have you learn from that day's reading.
Each book in the Financial Discipleship series focuses on a specific aspect of applying God's financial principles. This one will focus on preparing our hearts for eternity, so that we can fully enjoy all the Lord has waiting for us.
I'm dying to see what heaven will be like!

"What no eye has seen, nor ear heard, nor the heart of man imagined, what God has prepared for those who love him" (1 Corinthians 2:9).

Peter J. Briscoe, Leiden, The Netherlands, March 2023.

PART 1:

WELL DONE!

DAY 2: BEGIN WITH THE END IN MIND

KEY VERSE

"His master said to him, 'Well done, good and faithful servant. You have been faithful over a little; I will set you over much. Enter into the joy of your master.'"

Matthew 25:21

Well Done!

To be able to hear "Well done!" from the Master starts by keeping your end, your destiny, at the forefront of your vision. Beginning with the end in mind is all about determining your objectives in life and your motivation behind wanting them.

• What is my life purpose?
• Why am I trying to achieve this?
• What ideal outcomes am I looking for?
• Why are these important?
• Why am I about to do what I'm about to do?

Considering these questions means looking into your future and getting a vision of what that future should look like., People are mainly motivated by the future, and not the past. Seeing what your future should offer you. Is a great motivating factor and helps you to take the right decisions today. Dr. Stephen Covey said, "Your most important work is always ahead of you, never behind you."[1]

Beginning with the end in mind means planning each task or project with a clear view of your desired outcome, and then taking the right decisions to make that outcome reality.
It means to think about how you would like something to turn out before you get started. It moves your ideas in line with your future destiny.

In Lewis Carroll's classic, "Alice in Wonderland," Alice asks the Cheshire Cat, "Would you tell me, please, which way I ought to go from here?" "That depends a good deal on where you want to get to," said the Cat. "I don't much care where--" said Alice. "Then it doesn't matter which way you go," said the Cat. "-so long as I get somewhere," Alice added as an explanation. "Oh, you're sure to do that," said the Cat, "if you only walk long enough." [2]

The moral? How can you choose a road when you don't know

where you are headed? How can you get 'there' when you've no idea where 'there' is?

The better your perspective on the long-term, the better your decisions today. Being able to focus on your long-term purpose helps you to persevere, sacrifice, and pursue these goals. The apostle Paul's motivation to endure all he had to go through to achieve his goal was this: "I press on toward the goal for the prize of the upward call of God in Christ Jesus" (Philippians 3:14).

WHAT'S THE END?

God wants us to live our lives with the end in mind. He tells us what His end is for each of us and what our goal in life should be as a result. This is succinctly described in the Westminster confession. "The chief end of man is to glorify God and enjoy Him forever!" Because we live in the now, "forever" is a tough concept to grasp. We are locked into time and have trouble picturing what "forever" is like. The Bible tells us that "forever" is eternity, and heaven will be our dwelling place.

We don't exactly know what heaven will be like. It is difficult to describe what we have never seen or heard. It is so far beyond our comprehension or imagination.

The apostle Paul tells us about an experience he had – a vision of heaven. He says that he saw things that "cannot be told" (2 Corinthians 12:4).

It was impossible for him to describe what he had seen!

Jesus repeatedly used parables rather than direct descriptions to explain the kingdom. I think this indicates that the kingdom can't be communicated in human language.

When the Bible describes heaven, it is described in terms of what it is not. There will be no more mourning, no more hunger, crying, or pain. Our work will be no longer subject to the original curse due to sin. I fact, sin will not be present. Death will be no more. Imagine life without sin. We will enjoy perfect relationships with no disappointments, difficulties, or frustrations. We can't picture it, but it certainly should whet our appetites. We will see God face to face! We can eat from the tree of life! Nature will be restored, in all creation's beauty and fruitfulness. Just imagine the most exhilarating experience you have ever had and multiply that several times. That's heaven!

John gave us some insight. "Then the angel showed me the river of the water of life, bright as crystal, flowing from the throne of God and of the Lamb through the middle of the street of the city; also, on either side of the river, the tree of life with its twelve kinds of fruit, yielding its fruit each month. The leaves of the tree were for the healing of the nations. No longer will there be anything accursed, but the throne of God and of the Lamb will be in it, and his servants will worship him. They will see his face, and his name will be on their foreheads. And night will be no more. They will need no light of lamp or sun, for the Lord God will be their light, and they will reign forever and ever" (Revelation 22:1-5).

First, we see a river of the water of life flowing from the throne. It's a river – a constant supply of water. Water is essential for life and here it is a symbol of an overflowing, abundant life.

Then we see the tree of life to which we had no access after the Fall. The fruit of the tree of life brings healing to all nations – no more sickness, no more war. I believe there will still be nations, each with its own unique identity, but cooperating and enjoying what each has to offer in love and service

Lastly, we will rule together with Jesus forever and ever in the light of God on this earth! How awesome will this be? Jesus gives us a pretty good picture in Revelation 3:21 when He says to the people of Laodicea, *"Those who are victorious will sit with me on my throne, just as I was victorious and sat with my Father on his throne"* (NLT). We are no different than the Laodiceans. Those of us in today's world who finish well in Christ will be victorious for all of eternity. More about this on Day 3.

THE JOY OF THE MASTER!

The weddings of my three daughters are etched into my memory. What wonderful days full of joy for all who were invited – everyone dressed up in their finest, especially the lovely brides in white dresses (which cost me a small fortune but were worth every penny!).

Sometime, when the dead in Christ have risen to join those who are still living, we will be caught up into the air to meet the Lord. The Church will be invited to the wedding to end all weddings, the marriage feast of the Lamb!

"Then I heard what seemed to be the voice of a great multitude, like the roar of many waters and like the sound of mighty peals of thunder, crying out, 'Hallelujah!

For the Lord our God the Almighty reigns. Let us rejoice and exult and give him the glory, for the marriage of the Lamb has come, and his Bride has made herself ready; it was granted her to clothe herself with fine linen, bright and pure' – for the fine linen is the righteous deeds of the saints. And the angel said to me, 'Write this: Blessed are those who are invited to the marriage supper of the Lamb.' And he said to me, 'These are the true words of God'" (Revelation 19:6-10).

To attend this marriage feast, we need two sets of clothes. First is to be clothed with the righteousness of Christ, which is the free gift of God, cleansing us from all sin.

The second set is made from pure linen, *"the righteous deeds of the saints"* (Revelation 19:8). Both sets of clothes form the wedding garment, *"bright and pure."*

With the first set of clothes, Christ has made us ready for heaven. Right now we are preparing ourselves for heaven, getting ready for the *"joy of the master,"* the glory of the Bride – the Church, the body of Christ. Only Christ can give us the first set of clothes, but we must make the second set ourselves!

Anything we have done out of the right motive of a love for Christ and loving our neighbor as ourselves will qualify. Jesus said, *"Truly, I say to you, as you did it to one of the least of these my brothers, you did it to me"* (Matthew 25:40).

The supper of the wedding of the Lamb is better understood in the context of the marriage customs in the time of Christ. These

Jewish marriages usually developed over time, through three stages.
The first stage of this ancient Jewish marriage, is called, "Shiddukhin." In ancient times, it was the custom for the father of the groom to make an earnest effort to find a bride for his son. The parents of the bride and the groom then made up a marriage contract. The groom's parents or the groom himself then gave a dowry to the bride or her parents. This started what we would now call the betrothal period. This
was the time in Joseph and Mary's relationship that she became pregnant.

 We all, together, form the church, the Bride of Christ. The first phase of our union with Him was completed on earth when each individual believer placed his or her trust in Christ as Savior. The dowry paid by the father of the bridegroom (God the Father) was the blood that Christ shed on behalf of the bride. The contract was sealed with the Holy Spirit as a guarantee (see 2 Corinthians 5:5).

The second step was a continuation of the betrothal period in the ancient custom of *"Eyrusin."*
This process normally occurred a year later, when the groom, together with his male friends, visited the bride's house in a torchlight procession
at midnight. The bride, knowing in advance when this would happen, would be ready with her bridesmaids to join the procession. Together they would then go to the groom's ouse. This custom can be seen in parable of the ten bridesmaids in Matthew 25:1-13.

Under the *"huppah,"* the wedding veil, they then promise to marry each other and to keep the covenant or agreement. Here came the choice: to stay or run away – just as every human being can choose for or against Jesus. This already implied a loyalty to each other. A cup of wine was shared to close the covenant.
This cup points symbolically to the cup of the new covenant in the blood of Jesus. Whoever drinks from this is openly committing to be faithful to the agreement to marry later!

At this engagement party, the bride and groom were dressed in white, reflecting their purity.
The bride occupied herself for some time with her precious wedding garment, preparing it for the big day. During that time, the groom had time to build the house or put it in order. This house was always built on the land or property of the father.
The Church today is the "betrothed" of Christ. Like the wise bridesmaids in the parable, all believers should be alert and prepared for the appearance of the Bridegroom (the Second Coming.) This second phase finishes when Christ returns to claim His bride and take her to His Father's house.

The third and last stage was the *"nissuin,"* the bridal feast, which could last several days as indicated in the story of the wedding at Cana in John 2:1-2.
Following the betrothal feast, the bride wore a veil in public. This indicated two things: first, that she had already been bought and paid for by the bridegroom, and second, that she has come under the authority of her husband, unlike the unbelievers.
She also behaved differently from the other virgins in society.

In the time of Jesus, the father of the bridegroom gave permission to his son to pick up his bride only when everything was in order for the bridal chamber and the wedding feast. He gave the signal to go, with torches, shofars and music in loud procession to the bride's household to pick them up for the feast.
The vision of John in the book of Revelation is a depiction of the bridal feast of the Lamb (Jesus Christ) and His bride (the Church) in the third stage – the joy of the Master! I remember the great joy almost 50 years ago on the day I was married. I remember it as if it were yesterday. What a wonderful experience! To see my beautiful, lovely bride coming to me, so that we could be joined together by God in holy matrimony. Jesus will rejoice at seeing you at the party and you will be overawed!
If you are a Christian, then you are invited. The saints of old will be there – Abraham, Moses, David, Elijah … all rejoicing with us at the feast!

So, how are we preparing ourselves for this amazing event? We need to be doing the works that God has prepared for us. "For we are his workmanship, created in Christ Jesus for good works, which God prepared beforehand, that we should walk in them" (Ephesians 2:10).

Apart from entering the "joy of the master" at the wedding with the Lamb, we will finally be accepted in perfect and complete unity to reign with Christ. "Beloved, we are God's children now, and what we will be has not yet appeared; but we know that when he appears we shall be like him, because we shall see him as he is. And everyone who thus hopes in him purifies himself as he is pure" (1 John 3:2-3).

PREPARING FOR THE END?

Pleasing God starts with belief: to believe that God is who He says He is, to obey what He asks us to do, to develop a close relationship with Him, and to look forward to the rewards He promises for those who seek Him. Hebrews 11:6 says, "And without faith it is impossible to please him, for whoever would draw near to God must believe that he exists and that he rewards those who seek him."
It all boils down to Jesus' command to love God more than anything, and love others as we love ourselves. (Mark 12:30–31).

Loving God means to worship Him and Him alone. It means to allow the priorities of the kingdom to influence and determine our every decision.
It means to obey all He has commanded us to do. It means to be faithful stewards of all He has entrusted to us, using His resources, for His purposes in His way.
Loving others means to give, to serve, to help, so that they can reach their full potential as sons and daughters of God.
It means to share the gospel with them, both in word and deed. It means helping them become disciples, fully devoted followers of Jesus. Living in view of eternity should drastically change our lives.

People are so valuable to God that they span the gap between time and eternity. Paul writes, *"For what is our hope or joy or crown of boasting before our Lord Jesus at his coming? Is it not you?"* (1 Thessalonians 2:19) We are His most highly sought-after children. To love those who are His, to invest in their spiritual well-being, is to invest in what God is looking for most of all – His people. God's people are His most highly prized possession. To love those who are His, to invest in their spiritual well-being, is to attract special consideration.
What does a Christian living in view of eternity look like?

- In view of eternity, financial disciples have a focused prayer life.
- In view of eternity, financial disciples love other believers deeply.
- In view of eternity, financial disciples use their spiritual gifts to glorify God.
- In view of eternity, financial disciples are good stewards of the resources entrusted to them.
- In view of eternity, financial disciples help others know Christ and make Him known.

It is interesting to note that the reward for good stewardship is more stewardship! More responsibility. "You have been faithful with little; I will set you over much" (Matthew 25:23).
Really, the end is just the beginning!

A MOTIVATOR

Living in view of eternity can be a powerful backward-planning motivator as we start with the end in mind. We determine what we want to become in the end and what we want to be doing in the end, and we work backward to determine what we must do between now and then to achieve that goal. Establishing that goal provides a powerful sense of purpose for us on a day-to-day basis. It gives us the resolve to work hard when we are tired, to be resilient when we experience setbacks and failures, to be quick to repent and quick to forgive, and to focus on the future rather than the present.

Brandon Sieben, CEO of Compass – finances God's Way, tells of a lesson learned while studying for his MBA. The lesson was, "Look forward and reason back." He was taught to lay out a three-to-five-year strategic plan and then back up into what he should be doing in this quarter, the next quarter, and so on. A phrase he remembers is, "Invest for the long term while managing for the short term."

In concluding, we see how our faithfulness on earth results in greater responsibility in heaven. Christ will judge us on that basis.

If He can trust us with little, he can trust us with much!!

DAY 2: QUESTIONS TO PONDER.

How will your view on eternity affect decisions and choices you make today?

How do you see the purpose of your life and what you are trying to achieve?

What outcomes are you looking for? Why are these important to you?

DAY 3: ACCOUNTABILITY

KEY VERSE

"For we must all appear before the judgment seat of Christ, so that each one may receive what is due for what he has done in the body, whether good or evil."

2 Corinthians 5:10

A ccountability means to be willing and able to give an answer to those requiring information about what you have done, are doing or hope to do. It means carrying out the responsibilities we have been entrusted with, in all honesty, openness and transparency. Accountability is very important many people have problems with it. It seems the higher people climb the more difficult the accountability!

Accountability is extremely important to God and the Bible teaches a lot about the topic with examples of those who were accountable and those who were not.
The definition of accountability as expressed in the Bible comes from Romans 14:12, *"So then each of us will give an account of himself to God."*
Everyone is ultimately accountable to God. He is the Creator of all things. "And there is no creature hidden from His sight, but all things are open and laid bare to the eyes of Him with whom we have to do" (Hebrews 4:13, NASB1995).

In view of what Romans 14:12 states, when we die, we will all arrive at the Judgement Seat of Christ and give an account of what we did with the life we have been given. If we are found faithful and have used what we have been given in His way, we will hear the blessed recognition from Jesus, "*Well done, good and faithful servant*" (Matthew 25:23).

Jesus talked about accountability in Matthew 12:36 "I tell you, on the day of judgment people will give account for every careless word they speak, for by your words you will be justified, and by your words you will be condemned."
What we say and how we say it can make or break others and ourselves. On the day of judgment, we will be reminded of these words. We should not think that we will automatically be fine when we stand before God.

TEST

 Since we will all be judged by the Righteous One, it is important to evaluate our lives. Scripture teaches us, "Test yourselves to see if you are in the faith; examine yourselves! Or do you not recognize this about yourselves, that Jesus Christ is in you – unless indeed you fail the test?" (2 Corinthians 12:5, NASB).
Do you see changes in your life? The Bible says, "Therefore if anyone is in Christ, he is a new creature; the old things passed away; behold, new things have come" (2 Corinthians 5:17, NASB1995).
Only the life of Christ in us will provide the transforming power needed to live a life pleasing to the Lord.

Ask yourself these kinds of questions: [3]

- Are you walking in the light of God's truth and righteousness? (1 John 1:5–7).
- Are you daily confessing sin? (1 John 1:8–10).
- Do you obey Christ? (1 John 2:3–4).
- Do you love fellow Christians? (1 John 2:9–11).
- Do you hate worldliness? (1 John 2:15–17).
- Are you persevering in doctrine? (1 John 2:24–25).
- Are you practicing righteousness? (1 John 3:10).

- Do you see the fruit of the Spirit in your life? (Galatians 5:16–24).
- Are you growing under God's discipline? (Hebrews 12:5–8).
- Are you doing good works because of your salvation? (Ephesians 2:8–10).

How are you doing with the answers to these tough questions? If you can answer yes to them, you and people around you are seeing a substantial difference in your life. The Holy Spirit is changing you to become like Jesus. You are being transformed into Christlikeness. The biblical word used for "transformed" is *"metamorphoo"* from which we get our word "metamorphosis," used to describe the transformation process from a tiny egg to a beautiful butterfly. The end is a person of beauty, just like Jesus!

JUDGMENT

 When visiting the ancient city of Corinth, I would say the most moving spot of all is the raised stone platform called the bema. In ancient Greece, the bema was typically located at the center of the forum or marketplace where officials gave public addresses and heard legal cases,

The bema was raised platform in the assembly where speeches were given, and crowns were awarded to winners of the games. In ancient Rome, the Caesars sat on a 'bema' to reward those who had been victorious in battle.
As I stood there, the awesomeness of the moment overtook me, and I saw myself on a future day standing at Christ's throne. The Bible says, "For we must all appear before the judgment seat (bema) of Christ, so that each one may receive what is due for what he has done in the body, whether good or evil" (2 Corinthians 5:10).
All other courts or tribunals pale into insignificance before the bema of Christ. There we will be judged by a righteous Judge who knows and sees everything. "And no creature is hidden from his sight, but all are naked and exposed to the eyes of him to whom

we must give account." (Hebrews 4:13)

The judgment seat of Christ will take place after Christ returns and gathers believers to be with Him. Christ will evaluate our works and will reward us for faithfully serving Him. This is not a judgement to determine our eternal destination. That has been settled when we come to faith in Christ, accept Him and are born again by the Holy Spirit.

.Jesus told his beloved John in Revelation 22:12, "Behold, I am coming soon, bringing my recompense with me, to repay each one for what he has done." Believers are judged at the judgment seat of Christ (see Romans 14:10-12). Every believer will give an account of himself, and the Lord will judge the choices we have made.

This judgment does not determine salvation, which is by faith alone, but is the time when believers have to give an account of their lives in service to Christ.

THE BASIS FOR JUDGMENT

 What is the reference point by which we shall be judged at the bema? Jesus commended the stewards who had done well with the funds they had been given to work with: *"Well done, good and faithful servant."*

From the commendation Jesus gave to the stewards who had used the funds well, we can detect two criteria on which we will be judged. The first criterion is goodness, and the second, faithfulness. These will be discussed further in Part 2, Days 13 and 14.

Paul uses the metaphor of a building in his first letter to the Corinthians. *"For we are God's fellow workers. You are God's field, God's building"* (1 Corinthians 3:9). He explains that the foundation of the building is Jesus Himself. We have been given the privilege of working together with God to build the kingdom. God encourages His fellow workers, *"Let each one take care how he builds upon it" [the foundation]* (1 Corinthians 3:10). We must not take this privilege lightly.

Then Paul goes on to explain that we will be evaluated on how we build and with what kinds of materials. "Now if anyone builds on the foundation with gold, silver, precious stones, wood, hay, straw – each one's work will become manifest, for the Day will disclose it, because it will be revealed by fire, and the fire will test what sort of work each one has done. If the work that anyone has built on the foundation survives, he will receive a reward. If anyone's work is burned up, he will suffer loss, though he himself will be saved, but only as through fire" (1 Corinthians 3:12-15).

I believe that the "Day" Paul mentions is the day we will appear before the judgment seat of Christ. The fire of His holiness will test the quality of the work we have been doing. When John was given the privilege to see Jesus in glory, he wrote, "His eyes were like a flame of fire" (Revelation 1:14). "His face was like the sun shining in full strength" (Revelation 1:16).

Building with gold, silver, and precious stones are the works I believe God has prepared for us to do. *"For we are his workmanship, created in Christ Jesus for good works, which God prepared beforehand, that we should walk in them"* (Ephesians 2:10). This foundation has little to do with quantity (you can hold these gems and minerals in the palm of your hand) but more with quality: that which is done in obedience to Christ and out of a love for Him. I also believe that the *"treasures in heaven"* we are told to store up for ourselves will count in this regard.

John Bunyan, writing *The Pilgrim's Process* from a prison cell, stated, "Whatever good thing you do for Him, if done according to the Word, is laid up for you as treasure in chests and coffers, to be brought out to be rewarded before both men and angels, to your eternal comfort." 4

Building with an impressive pile of combustible materials, however good they may look in the eyes of the world, will not last a few seconds in the holiness of the fire. These represent *"treasures on earth,"* which Jesus tells us not to store up for ourselves.

David Livingstone, the Scottish explorer and missionary to Africa, said, "I place no value on anything I possess, except in relation to the kingdom of God." 5

In Part 2 of this book, Day 17, I discuss what Paul calls *"the works of the flesh,"* which also constitute flammable materials destined to be burned.

Our thoughts and intentions will be judged: *". . . discerning the thoughts and intentions of the heart. And no creature is hidden from his sight, but all are naked and exposed to the eyes of him to whom we must give account"* (Hebrews 4:12-13).

Our spoken words will be judged. "I tell you, on the day of judgment people will give account for every careless word they speak, for by your words you will be justified, and by your words you will be condemned" (Matthew 12:36-37).

Our motives will be judged. "Therefore do not pronounce judgment before the time, before the Lord comes, who will bring to light the things now hidden in darkness and will disclose the purposes of the heart. Then each one will receive his commendation from God" (1 Corinthians 4:5).

At the judgment seat of Christ, justice will be done and truth revealed.

When I think about this judgment, it really motivates me to take my responsibility seriously to steward all God has entrusted to me. I want to daily ask the Spirit to produce the fruits of righteousness in me, including my responsibility to pour Christ's love into the lives of others.

Earl Radmacher says, "The person I am becoming today, is preparing me for the person I shall be for all of eternity." We should be all that we can be on earth so that we can be all that we could be in heaven!

The apostle John was given a vision into the end times. He wrote, "And I heard a voice from heaven saying, 'Write this: Blessed are the dead who die in the Lord from now on.' 'Blessed indeed,' says the Spirit, 'that they may rest from their labors, for their deeds follow them!'" (Revelation 14:13). Our deeds on earth will not be lost or forgotten; they follow us, even after death, into eternal life.

TEARS IN HEAVEN?

 Pastor Erwin Lutzer, as senior pastor of Moody Bible Church, gave some helpful insights. [6]."Tears in heaven! In the minds of many Christians, tears and heaven simply do not belong together. Like war and peace, light and darkness, health and sickness, the Spirit and the flesh, these seem incompatible. But I believe there are good reasons why there will be tears in heaven. When we reflect on how we lived for Christ, who purchased us at such high cost, we may well weep on the other side of the celestial gates. Our tears could be those of regret and shame, tears of remorse for lives lived for ourselves rather than for *"Him who loves us and released us from our sins by His blood"* (Revelation 1:5, NASB). If we do not experience tears, then there would be no reason for the Lord to *"wipe away every tear from their eyes,"* as it is written in Revelation 21:4.

Of course, we could also experience tears of joy as we are overwhelmed by God's mercy and grace.
Pastor Lutzer, [7] "Perhaps we would never cease crying in heaven if God Himself did not come and wipe the tears from our eyes (Revelation 21:4). A friend of mine balked when I suggested that some people might experience deep regret along with lost privileges at the judgment seat of Christ. For him, the judgment seat of Christ is really no judgment at all – all believers will pass the judgment seat with flying colors. Not so. Let us hear the words of Paul. *"For we must all appear before the judgment seat of Christ, so that each one may be recompensed for his deeds [done] in the body, according to what he has done, whether good or bad"* (2 Corinthians 5:10, NASB).

That phrase, *"whether good or bad,"* rids us of the cherished hope that our failures can never return to haunt us. It reminds us that our

Father in heaven judges us even though we are secure in the knowledge that we are His children forever."
We should not conclude that every Christian will do well at the judgment seat of Christ. We can suffer loss of rewards, and many of us may stand in shame before Christ as we see our lives pass before us. We've already learned some lessons that should affect the way we live.

First, keep in mind that
this life is training for the next. We are to be learning the rules of the kingdom; we are apprentices for something better.
God's purpose is to mature us in faithfulness and service so that we will be a credit to Him on earth and a companion for Christ in heaven. Second, every day we live is either a loss or a gain so far as our future judgment is concerned. How we live today will help determine the words we hear from Christ tomorrow. Remember, the person we are today will determine the rewards we receive in the future. We can lose
our rewards both by the sins we commit and the opportunities we squander.

In the parable of the pounds, or minas (Luke 19:11-27), we read of a servant who wasted his opportunities, feared failure, and neglected to do what was commanded. He was condemned and had the money taken from him. He lost the approval of his master, faced temporary rejection, and was denied the opportunity to rule in the kingdom.
It is interesting to note that in the parable of the pounds, in which sums of money were given to ten servants, only three eventually showed up to give account of how they had used the money given to them. What happened to the other seven?

Personally, I think that we are the other seven servants. Our story is still being told. The Lord is watching what we do and evaluating our motives and outcomes. The end of our story won't be written until we stand before the Lord and He judges us for how we have used all the gifts He has entrusted to us.

REWARDS

Your faith determines your eternal destination, but your behavior determines your eternal rewards. As a believer, you are guaranteed an inheritance, based on your adoption into God's family as His child: it is eternal life with the Trinity! Your rewards are based on your actions.
Salvation is a free gift, given by God. Rewards are given for faithfulness in the Christian life or rewards can be withheld for unfaithfulness. Eternal rewards should be one of the great motivators of the Christian's life!!
The great Bible teacher, Ray Fowler, writes that "your reward will correspond to what you have been building in this life. If you have been living for God and Christ and His kingdom, then what you have built will survive into the next life." [18]

I like what N.T. Wright says about this in his book, *Surprised by Hope*.[9] He writes, "It isn't a matter of calculation, of doing a difficult job in order to be paid a wage. It is much more like working at a friendship or a marriage to enjoy the other person's company more fully."
He goes on to say that it's somewhat like practicing golf when you experience the joy of a good shot that results from the time put in at the practice range. "The 'reward' is organically connected to the activity, not some kind of arbitrary pat on the back, otherwise unrelated to the work that was done.

And it is always far in abundance beyond any sense of direct or equivalent payment.... The resurrection means that what you do in the present, in working hard for the gospel, is not wasted."
The rewards we will be given serve to equip us for the responsibilities we will be given in eternity when we are to *"rule with Christ."*
We will discuss more about rewards in Day 3.

DAY 3: QUESTIONS TO PONDER

What comes to mind when thinking about having to appear before the judgment seat of Christ?

What does "investing for the long term while managing for the short term" look like for you?

What does building on a foundation of "gold, silver, and precious stones" mean to you?

What trials and temptations have you been able to overcome? What remains a challenge?

DAY 4: REWARDS

KEY VERSE

"Look! I am coming soon, and my reward is with me to pay each one according to what he has done!"

Revelation 22:12

Most Christians have never thought much about life in eternity. This is surprising because the Bible gives us wonderful glimpses of what it will be like. Of course, we cannot fully grasp the enormity of it. I have found that having a clear view of what our *"treasures in heaven"* will include is a strong motivating factor to live for Christ in tough times and a reason to forego the *"treasures on earth"* that seem so very attractive.

Consider the biblical saints who were driven to serve God because of the prospect of a reward.
Abraham was willing to leave the security of Ur and live in tents without knowing where he was going because "he was looking for the city which has foundations, whose architect and builder is God" (Hebrews 11:10, NASB). This promise motivated him to obey God even though he died without the promise being fulfilled. He was rewarded in the life to come.
Moses was willing to leave the treasures of Egypt and defy the Pharaoh, "choosing rather to be mistreated with the people of God than to enjoy the fleeting pleasures of sin. He considered the reproach of Christ greater wealth than the treasures of Egypt, for he was looking to the reward" (Hebrews 11:25–26).

Paul was very concerned that he might be disqualified in the race of life. "I discipline my body and keep it under control, lest after preaching to others I myself should be disqualified." (1 Corinthians 9:27). He urged believers in Philippi to prove themselves to be blameless the midst of a 'crooked and twisted generation,' "holding fast to the word of life, so that in the day of Christ I may be proud that I did not run in vain or labor in vain." (Philippians 2:16).

Paul was encouraging believers to do well in the light of "the day of Christ."" Paul mentions is the eternal destiny of his readers, beginning at the bema, the judgment seat of Christ, where the works of believers will be judged to determine their eternal rewards.

GOD'S REWARDS

 When we consider that the ultimate reward is to rule with Christ as a joint heir, together charged with the responsibility of authority over all God's possessions, it is clear that such rewards are never earned in the usual sense of the word. God promises to give us rewards, but this is only because of His grace. We can demand nothing; indeed, after we have done our best, we are still unworthy servants, having *done only that which we ought to have done* (Luke 17:10, NASB). God has chosen to give us what we have no right to either demand
or expect. We are rewarded out of His generosity, not as an obligation.

His grace permeates our whole life; without His grace we would be utterly lost. However, after showering us with His unmerited favor, He does expect a response. As Augustine said, "without God we cannot; without us, He will not." [10] The initiative and work come entirely from God, and we react in response to and in cooperation with Him. Augustine continued, "He who created you without your help will not save you without your cooperation."

Pastor Lutzer continues, [11] "God expects us to work alongside Him to "work out your own salvation with fear and trembling, for it is

God who works in you, both to will and to work for his good pleasure" (Philippians 2:12-13). That is grace: not only does He save us from ourselves but also empowers us to work in such a way that He can say "Well done!"

It is important to realise that rewards are not given on the basis of a day's pay for a day's work. God's reward will be completely out of proportion to the work we have done. He has promised to reward us. If He didn't reward us, the author of Hebrews says, He would be "unjust." "For God is not unjust so as to overlook your work and the love that you have shown for his name in serving the saints, as you still do" (Hebrews 6:10).)."

Melanchthon, Luther's confidant and a theologian himself, made an important distinction between works prior to salvation, which lack merit, and those after conversion, which he calls "meritorious," the quality of being particularly good or worthy. He wrote, 12 "We teach that good works are meritorious – not for the forgiveness of sins, grace, nor justification (for we obtain these only by faith) but for other physical and spiritual rewards in this life and in that which is to come, as Paul says, "Each will receive his wages according to his labor" (1 Corinthians 3:8). Therefore, there will be different rewards for different labors; there will be distinctions in the glory of the saints.

Our relationship with God is much more that being a servant. It is more like a son or daughter who is loved by a father, who delights in giving him or her good things. When we are with the Lord in heaven, sin will be no more and we will be able to use the gifts and rewards given in an optimal way, to the glory of the Father and to the benefit of our neighbors. These gifts and rewards will be so unimaginably generous that we will praise God for all eternity!

NEW LEADERSHIP

 Before sin ever entered the world, God gave a command to Adam and Eve. He told them to be fruitful and multiply. Fill the earth and subdue it. He then gave them "dominion" over everything in this creation (see Genesis 1:28). God's command to Adam and Eve was a command to take up leadership.

Dominion, in an unfallen world, meant to lead the world – not in an oppressive and destructive manner but to reflect the love and leadership of God to it. From the beginning, God gave humanity the authority and responsibility to rule over the world.

This was a call to leadership from the day God created humanity. That plan got messed up when we sinned. Just because it went awfully wrong in the Garden doesn't mean it will stay that way for all eternity.

Christ-centered leadership will appear when Jesus comes again to earth to reign in a period of a thousand years in what is called the millennial kingdom. We, the body of Christ, will reign with him! The millennial kingdom is the title given to the thousand- year reign of Jesus Christ on the earth. Six times in Revelation 20:2-7, the millennial kingdom is specifically said to be a thousand years in length. Theologians have differing interpretations of this millennium. Does it literally refer to a thousand-year reign? When will it occur in relation to the second coming of Christ? A discussion on the merits of differing views is beyond the scope of this book.

Personally, I follow the teaching of the great preacher C. H. Spurgeon, who is quoted as saying; "If I read the word aright, and it is honest to admit that there is much room for difference of opinion here, the day will come, when the Lord Jesus will descend from heaven with a shout, with the trump of the archangel and the voice of God. I believe that Christ will come first; and *then* will come the millennium as the result of his personal reign upon earth. Be this the case or not, the fact is that Christ will suddenly come, come to reign, and come to judge the earth in righteousness." [13]

Leadership with Christ will not carry with it all the perversions that have come from sin. There won't be power mongering or greed or self-focused competition. There will be leadership in the most God-honoring, Christ-focused, and Spirit- empowered ways we can imagine. In fact, I don't know if we can imagine how leadership will be in a world that doesn't include sin or any of its effects. Leadership will be pure, unadulterated servanthood. It will fully reflect the servanthood of Christ, who loved us and gave Himself for us. To be a servant means to seek the best for the people you help, so that they can reach their maximum potential and fully participate in the life of the Trinity.

POSITIONS OF AUTHORITY

Consider these verses, beginning with a prophecy in the Son of Man passage in Daniel that will be fulfilled when Christ returns in his kingdom. "But the saints of the Most High will receive the kingdom and will possess it forever – yes, for ever and ever… Then the sovereignty, power and greatness of the kingdoms under the whole heaven will be handed over to the saints, the people of the Most High. His kingdom will be an everlasting kingdom, and all rulers will worship and obey him" (Daniel 7:18, 27, NIV1996, emphasis added).

Several passages indicate that we will rule with Christ in positions of authority in the new kingdom. This is fully in line with the greater responsibility given to the faithful servants in the parable of the talents, and also the ten cities given the faithful servant in the parable of the pounds or minas. In the parable of the minas, the Lord rewards His servants in accordance with the quantity of return produced from equal gifts. In the somewhat similar parable of the talents (Matthew 25:14-30), the reward is based on proportionate return from unequal gifts.

In the parable of the pounds, the nobleman went *"into a far country"* (Luke 19:12). In the parable of the talents, Jesus gives the additional information that the master returned *"after a long time"* (Matthew 25:19). Talents and pounds represent an opportunity for service. The rewards given are in terms of *"ruling over cities."* The conclusion[4] from the two parables is that the rewards we

receive when Christ returns are based on both quantitative and qualitative criteria. With full understanding, the Lord
will take account of our opportunities, our works, and the outcomes we deliver. What is clear from both parables is that Christ does expect a return on the gifts He has entrusted to us, whether it be in the multiplication of His word, the advancement of His kingdom into the lives of others, or
the increase in talents/pounds from what He initially and generously gives us. All of it, and specifically the reward to the two servants, was based on their faithful multiplication of fruit for Christ (the master).
He is well able to discern and "to give to every one according to his work" (Revelation 22:12).

MANAGING CITIES

Could you rule a city in the Messianic Kingdom? This question was well answered by an article from "Hope of Israel Ministries," which is reproduced here. [14]

With a voice more powerful than the most powerful waterfall but full of warmth and enthusiasm, the Messiah says the words you have been waiting to hear. In my paraphrase, "Well done, you good and faithful servant. You have been faithful in the things I gave you to do; you have overcome and you have endured to the end. Welcome to the kingdom of God, where I will give you even greater things to do. You shall have authority over ten cities" (Luke 19:17).

Did you ever stop to think about what must be done to manage a city or even a small town? Water and power must be provided, streets and roads have to be planned, and a building code must be established. Garbage must be collected. Disposal of sewage must be arranged. And what about transportation, a school system, shops, and places of entertainment? Taxes must be collected and the funds appropriated for the thousands of expenses needed to keep a town running properly. What do you know about all that? Some of the best minds in the world today can't make our towns and cities work. So what makes you think you are going to do any better in the world tomorrow?

The book of Revelation shows how the trumpet plagues and the events leading up to the Messiah's future appearance will devastate civilization. Communication networks will be in ruins. Transportation will have broken down. Dams will have been destroyed and bridges will have collapsed. Once-great cities will be nothing but smoking piles of rubble. The ecosystem will have been badly damaged. But, starting from Jerusalem, the healing and rebuilding will commence. Representatives of once proud nations will make their way to Jesus' seat of government, to be taught His ways and walk in His paths (Isaiah 2:3).

God does not need to see you in action on a large scale to determine whether you know how to administer the laws that lead to peace. He sees it now in the way you solve the problems of your own life. Every day brings a thousand and
one little decisions that show God whether you are learning His way or not. You must work to develop the attributes of a king by yielding to the will of God (see Matthew 7:21, 18:3, and James 1:22-25). To be a ruler in the future, you must look beyond the difficulties now facing you, to your ultimate reward (see Romans 8:18). That is what Jesus did (see Hebrews 12:2-3, I Peter 2:21).

MANAGING NATIONS

Our end is also described in this way; ". . . by your blood you ransomed people for God from every tribe and language and people and nation, and you have made them a kingdom and priests to our God, and they shall reign on the earth" (Revelation 5:9-10). That's why we need to disciple people – so they can become fit to "reign on earth."
The Bible tells us that Jesus will return and will reign on earth for a thousand years – and we with Him! ". . . they will be priests of God and of Christ, and they will reign with him for a thousand years" (Revelation 20:6).

Jesus' thousand-year reign on earth is the kingdom of God, of heaven, and is that which the dead and alive in Christ will inherit "at his coming" (1 Corinthians 15:23), when "the Lord himself will descend from heaven with a shout" (1 Thessalonians 4:16, NKJV). Yes, when this happens, these resurrected saints will rule over cities and nations: we "shall reign on the earth . . . over the nations" (Revelation 5:10, 2:26). Jesus also promised this when he said, "Blessed are the meek, for they shall inherit the earth" (Matthew 5:5).

God's people will have authority over the nations in the millennial reign: "Then the sovereignty, power, and greatness of the kingdoms under the whole heaven will be handed over to the saints, the people of the Most High. His kingdom will be an everlasting kingdom, and all rulers will worship and obey him" (Daniel 7:27, NIV1996, emphasis added).
This passage speaks of the Son of Man (Jesus' favorite name for Himself), whom Daniel prophesized would be the ruler of the universe in the end times. Under the Son of Man's rule, the "sovereignty, power and greatness of the kingdoms… will be handed over to the saints."

The Lord revealed to John, "To him who overcomes and keeps my works to the end, I will give authority over the nations" (Revelation 2:26, MEV, emphasis added).
God will give us authority over the nations! In the new heaven and new earth, every tribe, tongue, nation, and people group will be represented (see Revelation 7:9). And God's people – who are from every nation – will have authority over the nations.

Just think, no more political corruption in the newspapers! No bribery, kickbacks, or broken promises! We will be able to get the King to solve all our problems without Satan's interventions.
That is why a Christian can be an optimist. That is why a Christian can smile in the midst of all that is currently happening. We know what will come for us. We know what the end will be – the triumph of the Lord Jesus Christ! *The kingdoms of this world* have become

the kingdoms of our Lord and of his Christ; and he shall reign forever and ever" (Revelation 11:15, NKJV).

SPURGEON

To end this Day's reading, I would like to insert a lengthy quote from the great preacher, Charles Haddon Spurgeon, known as the "prince of preachers." [15]The boundless regions of the Father's universe belong to Christ. He has been given an eternal right to them. He is the sole Owner of the vast creation of God; He is the Heir of all things.
Because we are co-heirs with Him, we too may regard all things as our own. The golden streets of paradise, the pearly gates, the river of life, the endless bliss and unspeakable glory, yes everything has been given to us by our blessed Lord for our eternal possession. All that He has, He shares with His people.
He has put a royal crown on the head of His Church. He uncrowned Himself in order to crown us with glory. He did not want to take a place on His own throne before He had won a place for all those who would overcome through His blood. When the Head is crowned, the whole Body shares in the honor.
See here the reward for every Christian victor! Christ's throne, crown, palace, clothes, treasures and inheritance, everything is ours. Christ is infinitely
superior to jealousy and selfishness. He is not selfish. He makes others partakers of His privileges. I have given them the glory that You have given Me.

The manifestations of His Father's love are even more glorious to Him, because His people share them with Him. The glory of His kingdom rejoices in Him even more, because His people will be seen with Him in
His glory. The victories He has won are of even greater value to Him, because they have taught His people to overcome. He rejoices in His royal garment, because His hems cover His children. He enjoys His joy even more, because He calls His people to enter into this joy.

DAY 4: QUESTIONS TO PONDER

47

Think about Augustine's words, "Without God we cannot; without us, He will not." How do you see God's part and your part working out in your Ife?

What comes to mind when you think of God's rewards?

What are you doing now that may have an impact on the rewards you receive?

What do you think it will be like to be like Christ?

DAY 5: TREASURES IN HEAVEN

KEY VERSE

"They are to do good, to be rich in good works, to be generous and ready to share, thus storing up treasure for themselves as a good foundation for the future, so that they may take hold of that which is truly life."

1 Timothy 6:18-19

J esus Himself spoke many times of rewards or something great that we could look forward to – especially these rewards of "treasures in heaven." What are these "treasures in heaven"?

Well, first I believe we can look forward to an intimate relationship with Jesus Christ and the privilege of hearing "Well done, good and faithful servant . . . Enter into the joy of your master." It has been said that all of life is a search for a perfect person in a perfect place. We will find this perfect person with whom we have this intimate relationship in the perfect place!

Second, the Bible says we will reign with Christ in positions of authority (as kings), fully equipped to participate first in the millennial reign of Christ on earth and later in what the Bible calls *"the new heavens and the new earth,"* where God is recreating this earth to be something perfect.

Jesus said, "Do not lay up for yourselves treasures on earth where moth and rust destroy and thieves break in and steal" (Matthew 6:19). He then gives us a command. "But lay up for yourselves treasures in heaven, where neither moth nor rust destroys and where thieves do not break in and steal" (Matthew 6:20). That is the kind of lasting investment He advises us to make. Then Jesus goes on to say, "For where your treasure is, there your heart will be also" (Matthew 6:21).

Those who know Jesus have received a wonderful perspective on eternity in heaven. Every time you send treasures to heaven, your heart moves in that direction, taking you ever closer to heaven. Furthermore, it refers to the place where those treasures are kept – the actual storehouse. We have to ask ourselves, Are we storing up precious things that will amount to something only on earth (temporary), or are we storing up real treasures that matter to God in heaven (forever)?
Jesus is referring to both realities: *what* believers store up, and *where* they store it – on a dying earth or in an eternal heaven.

CROWNS

Several verses in the New Testament indicate that all of God's people will receive crowns. These crowns signify royalty – kings or queens. Kings wore crowns. And kings have respect, authority, and power. The fact that you will receive a crown indicates that you will have dominion on the new earth.
An everlasting crown: "Everyone who competes in the games goes into strict training. They do it to get a crown that will not last, but we do it to get a crown that will last forever" (1 Corinthians 9:25, NIV, emphasis added).

A crown of righteousness: "Now there is in store for me the crown of righteousness, which the Lord, the righteous Judge, will award to me on that day – and not only to me but also to all who have longed for his appearing**" (2 Timothy 4:8,).

A crown of life: "Blessed is the one who perseveres under trial because, having stood the test, **t**hat person will receive the crown of life that the Lord has promised to those who love him" (James 1:12, NIV).

A crown of glory: "And when the Chief Shepherd appears, **you will receive the crown of glory** that will never fade away" (1 Peter 5:4, NIV).

A victors crown: "Do not be afraid of what you are about to suffer. I tell you, the devil will put some of you in prison to test you, and you will suffer persecution for ten days. Be faithful, even to the point of death, and **I will give you life as your victor's crown"** (Revelation 2:10, NIV).

The Romanian pastor Josef Ton, who overcame terrible persecutions at the hands of the Romanian communist secret police, points out that rewards, the crowns, are not merely decorative adornments in which we can take pride. He said, "The deepest reward is in the very fact that we will become what our Creator intends us to become. It is the reward of being made into the likeness of Christ. When we will be like Him, we will be qualified to share with Him in the inheritance, and to work with Him in important positions of high responsibility over the whole universe." [16]

Our salvation will become complete when we meet Jesus and become like Him. "Beloved, we are God's children now, and what we will be has not yet appeared; but we know that when he appears we shall be like him, because we shall see him as he is. And everyone who thus hopes in him purifies himself as he is pure" (1 John 3:2-3).

One of our dear Dutch Christian heroines is Corrie Ten Boom. Corrie used to carry a piece of embroidery around with her. She showed the underside, where all the knotted thread was visible, in a tangled, chaotic mess! Then she turned it over. On the front was a beautiful crown, embroidered with love and tender care. The Lord is busy in our lives, and the needle can sometimes be painful, but he is making something beautiful!

The goal of our salvation is not just to get us out of hell and into heaven. It is much more – it is to grow into Christlikeness. We are not there yet, but as Pastor Ray Steadman said, "We are all nuts, but the difference is, we are screwed onto the right bolt!"

Is this a motivation for you, as it is for me, to *"purify yourself,"* to live a life following Jesus and obeying His commands?

Will you allow me to imagine for a moment, what it means to be like Christ? Could I turn water into wine without a fermentation process? Walk on water with no boat? Heal the sick with no hospital? Give sight to the blind without
performing surgery? Multiply bread without having to build a bakery? Love someone with no selfishness whatsoever?
Just imagine . . .

TREASURES ON EARTH

"Treasures on earth" refer to various forms of money such as investments in mutual funds, stocks, bonds, and savings accounts as well as the accumulation of things that become like trophies, feeding our pride and greed instead of advancing Christ's kingdom in our life and the lives of others.
Many of these are riches we trust in to provide future security. It is so easy for our heart to emotionally lock into these things, making them our treasures. This is idolatry, trusting in something or someone other than Jesus Christ.

 Why not store up "treasures on earth"? First, it's just a poor investment. And in building our eternity portfolio, we want to have the best investments. Secondly, Jesus said that earthly treasures capture the human spirit. The things of the world tend to bind us to the world and take our focus off of God.
Thirdly, they will not last.

Why do I say building up "treasures on earth" is a poor investment? Jesus said "Do not lay up for yourselves treasures on earth, where moth and rust destroy and where thieves break in and steal, but lay up for yourselves treasures in heaven, where neither moth nor rust destroys and where thieves do not break in and steal." (Matthew 6:19)

Treasures on earth will be eaten away like rust and their usefulness destroyed. Jesus said moths can consume these investments – the forces of nature are unpredictable and unstable. Inflation can come in a single day. Deterioration and obsolescence are built into our economic life. Circumstances change. We lose our jobs. The things we have built our lives on can just crumble away. Thieves can break in and steal. We have to deal with dishonesty, greed, and deception that leads to loss of income. Joy is often stolen, and we become anxious, fearing loss as we experience the need to protect and preserve what we have. Other types of thieves are constantly threatening to steal our living: illness, business losses, depression, war, inflation, and finally, death itself. So focusing on "treasures on earth" is just a poor investment.

Secondly, it captures the human spirit. Jesus said, "For where your treasure is, there your heart will be also." We are created for something higher. We should instead be devoted to God and His plans for us because the kingdom is our inheritance. Esau, one of the sons of Jacob, sold his whole inheritance for a single meal; sometimes we sell a whole inheritance in the kingdom of God for "treasures on earth." Judas sold Jesus for money that led to his own death.

Thirdly, "treasures on earth" will not last. One of my favorite illustrations of this is Proverbs 23:5. You can just picture it. "When your eyes light on it [wealth], it is gone, for suddenly it sprouts wings, flying like an eagle toward heaven." Financial wealth is fleeting, it soon goes. Have you ever asked yourself, Where on earth did my money go? You cannot take it with you when you pass away into eternity. You never see a moving van behind a funeral procession. Pharaoh Tutankhamun thought he could take it with him. It didn't work then, and it won't work now!

For now, we need enough to get by – the rest we can send on ahead!

How can we identify treasures on earth? A. W. Tozer suggested we may discover the answer by responding to four basic questions: [17]

- What do we value most?
- What would we most hate to lose?
- What do our thoughts turn to most frequently when we are free to think of what we will?

- What affords us the greatest pleasure?"

If the things we value most are material things, then we are focused on "treasures on earth." What do you think of most? It's really a battleground for our heart. And the more we set our vision on eternity, on "treasures in heaven," the less our earthly treasures will hold a death grip on us.

Being focused on "treasures on earth" is idolatry, a violation of the first commandment: to love the Lord your God with all your being. Jesus described the competition for our devotion and the effect it has on our allegiance to God in Matthew 6:24. "No one can serve two masters, for either he will hate the one and love the other, or he will be devoted to the one and despise the other. You cannot serve God and money." Money can so easily become an idol if our hearts are focused on "treasures on earth."

"Treasures on earth" are temporary and fleeting. They will give only temporary satisfaction, temporary meaning. We need to focus on something else – on building up for ourselves "treasures in heaven," Jesus said, "Truly, I say to you, there is no one who has left house or wife or brothers or parents or children, for the sake of the kingdom of God, who will not receive many times more in this time, and in the age to come eternal life" (Luke 18:29-30).
Martin Luther King Jr. said, "As a young man with most of my life ahead of me, I decided early to give my life to something eternal and absolute. Not to these little gods that are here today and gone tomorrow. But to God who is the same yesterday, today, and forever." 18

THE RICH FOOL

The great painter Rembrandt knew what it was like to be rich and live a lavish lifestyle. He also knew what it was like to go bankrupt and lose it all. One of my favorite paintings hangs in a Berlin museum, in which Rembrandt describes the parable of the rich fool. Let's take a look at the painting.

 We see an elderly man has 'pince-nez' spectacles perched on his nose, sitting at a table which is overloaded with books and papers, some written in Hebrew. He is looking carefully at one of his gold coins.
.On the desk we can see scales to weigh the gold. A large book of accounts is opened as he tallies his treasure. The table is covered with many large books, which as Rembrandt pained this in the 17th century, symbolized pride.
He is clothed in expensive attire, reflecting his wealth.
But there are also details that indicate the fragility of this man. While there are magnifying glasses around him, which is another symbol of how wealthy he is, it also indicates that his eyesight is going. His eyes seem misted up and his glasses show that his vision is deteriorating. His whole face seems to reflect old age. Despite his wealth, his whole body is failing him.

I think that if Rembrandt were to paint this in our times, he would choose a wealthy banker in a sharp suit watching the Dow Jones index on one screen, his spreadsheet on the other, thinking on how to expand his wealth. There would be tablets strewn on his desk and a glass of whisky at hand. His face would show anguished stress lines as he ponders his portfolio.
This proud man is totally focused on his money.

Jesus told his listeners about a man who grew a bumper crop of grain. Too much of a good thing meant he had nowhere to store it. Instead of helping other people, he decided to build bigger barns. Then he could have years' worth of grain to sell. He could retire. In this story, there are 11 references (use of the words "I" or "my") to how this rich fool focused on himself. Count them!

I once heard a preacher lament, "It is curious how the popularity of this passage is inversely related to how much money the hearer has, being very much enjoyed by the poor but leaving the rich shifting uncomfortably in their seats!"

The rich fool thought, "What shall I do, for I have nowhere to store my crops? . . . I will do this: I will tear down my barns and build larger ones, and there I will store all my grain and my goods. And I will say to my soul, 'Soul, you have ample goods laid up for many years; relax, eat, drink, be merry.' But God said to him, 'Fool! This night your soul is required of you, and the things you have prepared, whose will they be?'"

Jesus concluded, "So is the one who lays up treasure for himself and is not rich toward God." (Read Luke 12:13-21.)
So what does it mean to be rich toward God? The Bible says, command them to do good, to be rich in good deeds, and to be generous and willing to share. It's no wonder that Augustine said, "The rich fool didn't realize the bellies of the poor were much safer storerooms than his barns."

And then Paul writes to Timothy, "As for the rich in this present age, charge them not to be haughty, nor to set their hopes on the uncertainty of riches, but on God, who richly provides us with everything to enjoy. They are to do good, to be rich in good works, to be generous and ready to share, thus storing up treasure for themselves as a good foundation for the future, so that they may take hold of that which is truly life" (1 Timothy 6:17-19).

BURIED TREASURE

It's a hot day. A traveler walks across sun-burned fields toward his business in the city. He carries a staff to help him on the long journey. All of a sudden, he pokes his staff into some softer earth and hits something hard. A box! *I wonder what's in there,* he thinks. He furtively looks around, sees no one there and pokes some more. He starts digging and unearths the box. His heart is pounding as he pries open the rusty lock and looks inside the chest. Treasure! Gold and precious jewels
– a fortune!
Overjoyed at finding such treasure, he wonders who owns the land. Can I afford to buy it? The man buries the treasure again and travels on to the city.

He decides to liquidate all his assets in order to buy the field containing the box of treasure. It's a risk, but one worth taking, he thinks to himself. He sells his farm and livestock, and with the proceeds he negotiates a good price with the owner of the field. It costs him everything he owns to gain everything that matters! Jesus tells this parable in two sentences. "The kingdom of heaven is like treasure hidden in a field, which a man found and covered up. Then in his joy he goes and sells all that he has and buys that field" (Matthew 13:44).

The parable could signify Jesus giving up all He had to gain the "treasure" of you and me. It could also be a reference to the immeasurable treasures in heaven that await us, making it more than worthwhile to sell all we have to gain them.
The rich, young leader who went to Jesus asking how to inherit eternal life got a reply he wasn't expecting (see Luke 18:18- 30). This religious person, claiming to have lived up to all the commandments, missed a huge one. Jesus laid His finger on the sore spot, and it hurt. Money was the young man's god; he was obsessed with earthy treasures. The remedy was, "Sell all that you have and distribute to the poor, and you will have treasure in heaven; and come, follow me" (verse 22). Unfortunately, the young leader went away sad "for he was extremely rich."

The disciples were listening and wondering how on earth they could get to heaven. Peter said, "See, we have left our homes and followed you" (verse 28). Jesus replied, "Truly, I say to you, there is no one who has left house or wife or brothers or parents or children, for the sake of the kingdom of God, who will not receive many times more in this time, and in the age to come eternal life" (verses 29-30). An investment made on earth will yield "treasures in heaven."

The rich, young man, who, according to Jewish historians was a Pharisee and member of the elite Sanhedrin, obviously did not know his Scriptures. He should have known Proverbs 19:17, *"Whoever is generous to the poor lends to the Lord, and he will repay him for his deed."* An investment in the poor will be paid back by God in some way at some time!

Realizing that I can lay up for myself *"treasures in heaven"* drives me to leave *"treasures on earth"* alone and trust the Lord for all I need to live on.

DAY 5: QUESTIONS TO PONDER

What do you understand to be "treasures on earth"?

Based on Tozer's suggestion for identifying "treasures on earth," how would you answer the following questions:
What do you value most?

What would you most hate to lose?

What does laying up "treasures in heaven" look like for you in the here and now?

DAY 6: LIVING IN THE LIGHT OF ETERNITY

KEY VERSE

"For this light momentary affliction is preparing for us an eternal weight of glory beyond all comparison, as we look not to the things that are seen but to
the things that are unseen. For the things that are seen are transient, but the things that are unseen are eternal."

1 Corinthians 4:17-18

I have been asked by a friend to explain eternity. "Well, I could," I replied, "but it would take forever!"

It is helpful to stand back and take a more objective perspective on life and what we are doing. We can be so consumed by everyday problems that we cannot seem to take a bird's eye view and evaluate our priorities. Someone quipped, "how can you drain a swamp when you are up to your neck in alligators?" The tyranny of the urgent stops us from looking objectively at what we are doing to see if we are still on track with what we should be doing. We become lost in the here and now and don't think of eternity and the eternal values that will outlive us. Everything you do today matters forever. God will live forever, people will live forever, and His word will live forever.

I have found Randy Alcorn's illustration of the dot and the line to be very helpful. The dot represents our years on earth, while the line represents eternity. Right now, all of us are living inside the dot.
Our present life on earth is the dot. It begins. It ends. It's brief. We are all living inside the dot. However, from the dot extends a line that goes on forever. That line is eternity, which Christians will spend in heaven. Right now, we're living in the dot, a

short window of opportunity, but everything we do inside the dot matters forever. What are we living for

The short-sighted person lives for the dot. In the dot, we are consumed with the cares of this world: how fine a house we can mortgage, how nice a car we can drive, what the latest fashion trends in clothing are, and how big we can build our retirement account.

The person with an eternal perspective lives for the line. In the line, we are preparing for an eternity with God, and this is affecting our daily "in the dot" decisions. Very few Christians think beyond the dot to the line – to the eternity that awaits us. How foolish it is to live for the dot that is only a blip on the screen of our eternal existence. The key is to live your life now

– while you're in the dot – in light of the line and investing in it. That's what's going to matter after you die.

Randy Alcorn says, "The people who change lives are the ones who point us away from the world's short-term perspective to God's long-term perspective. Very few Christians think beyond the dot to the line – to the eternity that awaits us. How foolish it is to live for the dot that is only a blip on the screen of our eternal existence. So live your life now, while you're in the dot, in light of the line, investing in the line." [19]

The dot and the line are interdependent; it's not either/or, but both/and. In this earthly life there's no way to not live in the dot. But we can prioritize the long game – focusing on the line with eternal goals, objectives, actions, and desired outcomes.

On the other hand, it's possible to become so focused on dreaming of eternity that we fail to live the life Jesus calls us to in the here and now. A few people I know could be described as "too heavenly minded and no earthly good."

Several hundred years ago a shipload of travelers landed on the northeast coast of America. The first year they established a town, the next year, a government. The third year, the government planned to build a road five miles into the wilderness. The fourth year, they tried to impeach the government because they thought it was a waste of money to build such a road. Here was a group of people who had the vision to travel thousands of miles and endure many hardships, but in just a few years had lost the vision to see even five miles into the wilderness.

Have you traveled many miles since first trusting Christ, even endured many hardships, but at present have lost your vision of eternal reward and how valuable it will be? Is it time to start living once again in light of eternity?

"Resolved, I will live so, as I wish I had done when I come to die."

These words were penned by nineteen-year-old Jonathan Edwards, who in 1722 kept a diary and wrote seventy guidelines, which he called "Resolutions." [20]

Jonathan Edwards resolved to live a life that would count in eternity, with God's help and grace in accordance to His will. He was daily aware of the reality of death and living before God with an eternal perspective. He considered the brevity of life to be important in his living and preaching. He knew well that life is a breath, *"a mist that appears for a little time and then vanishes"* (James 4:14). Just as life in Edwards's 18th century was frail and fragile, life continues to be frail and fragile today. Can we, too, live today as for eternity?

LIVING IN THE LIGHT OF ETERNITY

At midnight in Sydney as the year 2000 and the new millennium began, the word **Eternity** lit up on the Harbour Bridge. The backstory is the personal story of Arthur Stace. [21]

Born in poverty to alcoholic parents, he had little education and became a petty criminal, a homeless alcoholic. In the aftermath of World War 2, he joined the lines outside St Barnabas Broadway, an Anglican church in Sydney that provided food and shelter for the homeless. However, getting a meal involved first hearing a sermon.

Stace listened and turned to Jesus Christ. One night at another church, he heard a sermon on Isaiah 57:15. "For thus says the One who is high and lifted up, who inhabits Eternity, whose name is

Holy . . ." The preacher said, "I wish that I could sound or shout **Eternity** to everyone in the streets of Sydney. We've all got to meet it. Where will you spend Eternity?"
Taking up the challenge, the almost illiterate Arthur Stace started chalking "**Eternity**," in a distinctive copperplate script on the streets of Downtown Sydney. Over 35 years, he chalked it 500,000 times. **Eternity** became the mystery and the fascination of Sydney.

Just imagine walking through a door with an EXIT sign, not sure what you would find on the other side? That's what it will be like for many people at the end of their life as they exit earth and enter eternity. For most people, eternity is irrelevant – they live in the here and now, as they please. That's so sad, because our life here on earth is so short … eternity is, well, eternal. For us, as believers, living in the light of eternity has consequences.
First, knowing that we will spend eternity with Christ settled, gives us peace knowing that our salvation does not depend on anything I can do, but solely on what Christ has done on the cross

Second, we can joyously look forward to all heaven will bring. We will become free from this sinful, broken world and enter a Kingdom without suffering and abuse. It is not difficult to imagine why the writers of the Bible earnestly looked forward to that day when we can be with Jesus in eternity.

Last, living in the light of eternity, gives us a heightened sense of the commission we have been given to love people and help them along their path to eternity.

Are you living with a view of eternity? Are you living as though Christ could come back for you today? Living in the light of eternity gives us a different perspective of suffering. Peter wrote, "And after you have suffered a little while, the God of all grace, who has called you to his eternal glory in Christ, will himself restore, confirm, strengthen, and establish you." (1 Peter 5:10)
Peter is encouraging us to be focusing on the "eternal glory." Christ's ultimate goal is to remove all suffering, but while we are waiting, he promises to give us the strength to bear our current

sufferings and come out on top! He gives meaning to suffering –
to establish us in the faith. Peter knew suffering and persecution in
his lifetime two thousand years ago. Christians are still going
through the same today, but with the same hope as he had.
this was written, it is still as true for us today as it was then.

PREPARING FOR THE FUTURE

Jesus told his disciples a story. Let me paraphrase.

The manager has a tough job. He's the representative of the
richest guy in town and has to deal with all sorts of money- hungry
merchants and traders. The manager must combine the slippery
skills of a politician with the money savvy of an investor who
trades in commodity futures. If he pours too much of his master's
money in olive oil or wheat, and it's a bad year, then he'll be out of
a job. And back then there weren't many second chances – mess it
up and you're done. You can spend the rest of your life among the
expendable class, the beggars and common laborers. There isn't
another company or investment group to work for in town.
But apparently our friend the manager offends some of the town
traders enough for them to send nasty rumors to the boss. They
want the manager sacked; or maybe it's just the merchants
showing their strong arm to the manager – letting him know who's
really in charge.

The owner of the business calls the manager into his office and
angrily says, "What is this I hear about you? Turn in the books.
Explain your decisions. Give me an account of your management."
The boss then points his finger; "You're fired!"
The manager goes away and starts wondering how he is going to
survive without a job. I am not strong enough to work as a builder,
and I am ashamed to ask for social security or welfare.
He comes up with a brilliant plan. The business owner praises him
for showing streetwise wisdom. His plan is to reduce the debt
burden on two major customers, so they will be able to pay their
debts more easily. His motivation is clear: he wants to make
friends so they will be inclined to repay the favor. *I have decided*

what to do so that when I am removed from my management job, these people may receive me into their businesses.
When the boss gets the news of what the manager has done, he thinks it through and actually commends the manager for being shrewd. You can read the original story in Luke 16:1-8.

This parable is all about preparing for the future. The story is essentially concerned with our eternal destiny. This can be better understood by looking at a Greek word used by Luke in retelling the story. This word is *"methistemi,"* from which we get our medical word "metastasis." This means to change
place, to remove from one place to another. A patient goes to the doctor complaining about a lump, and after some tests, the doctor comes back with the terrible words, "It's cancer."
If things go from bad to worse, the doctor might inform the patient that the cancer has metastasized, meaning it has moved on to somewhere else in the body. So, our manager is being "metastasized," or moved on This gives an important hint at the meaning of our parable. Interestingly, Greeks today still use the word metastasis to indicate the removal of a person from this world to the next. If a Greek were to refer to his brother as his "metastasized" brother, any Greek would know immediately that he was speaking about his dead brother.
He has been metastasized: he has gone from this world to the next.

The manager is being removed from his job, an allusion to when we will be removed from this earth to face our Maker.
In this parable, the Lord is teaching us about a man who has been removed or metastasized from his job; the application to be made to ourselves is that we will all be metastasized from the world in which we now live.
The word *"methistemi"* is also used in Acts 13:22 by Luke (a doctor) to describe the removal of King Saul by God. It is also used by Paul to describe our salvation, which culminates
in our being "transferred to the kingdom of his beloved Son" (Colossians 1:13).

Our parable is all about getting prepared for future changes in our status – a future in which we are about to be removed from this world to meet our Maker and give account for
our lives.

We live on this earth for a determined number of years, after which everyone is "metastasized" into a new reality that lasts for eternity. Jesus wants us to get serious about preparing for eternity! The manager's thoughts were, of course, short term. After his dismissal, he wanted to get a new job as a manager somewhere else, but Jesus uses this story to focus
our attention on eternity. Preparing for the future is extremely important. If we don't prepare, the future becomes today before we are ready for it. We have so little time left to do what's important! Winston Churchill is quoted as saying, "The better the perspective on the future, the better your decisions will be today."

A pastor tells of when he was getting fuel for his car just before a holiday weekend. It was very busy, and he had a long wait.
He went to pay, and the attendant said apologetically, "Sorry you had to wait such a long time. It seems like people wait until the last minute before getting ready for a long journey."
"Yes, I know," replied the pastor, "I have the same problem in my profession, too!"

Jesus gives us the lesson of the parable by showing us how the manager prepared for his transition. "And I tell you, make friends for yourselves by means of unrighteous wealth, so that when it fails they may receive you into the eternal dwellings" (Luke 16:9). The idea of "being received into eternal dwellings" was, according to the Greek Lexicon, very common in ancient Greece.

In Berlin, the old Reichsmark was converted into a new currency, the Deutschmark in 1948. Reichsmarks become worthless and many people lost up to 90% of their wealth. The smart thing would have been to change their Reichsmarks into dollars or pounds, keeping only enough for their daily needs.

We can do the same by sending our money "on ahead," investing our money in kingdom work, building up for ourselves "treasures in heaven."

We can do this by sending our money "on ahead," investing money in kingdom work, building up for ourselves *"treasures in heaven."* Fortunately, that is not the end of the story. Jesus will eventually triumph and take us to a home he has prepared for us. "For we know that if the tent that is our earthly home is destroyed, we have a building from God, a house not made with hands, eternal in the heavens" (2 Corinthians 5:1). Mammon's influence will no longer be felt there. It is there that we desire to take people along with us and use our resources, our money, to bring as many people as possible to the eternal dwellings.

In our parable, Jesus is teaching us that we are all going to be *"metastasized"'* from this world into the next.

HOW THEN SHOULD I LIVE?

Martin Luther said, "I have two days on my calendar: this day and that Day." [22] John Wesley, the great preacher lived his life accordingly. He echoed Luther when he said, "I value all things only by the price they shall gain in eternity." [23]

The standard by which they measured all their activities and priorities was their impact on eternity.

Uncle Screwtape, a fictional demon from C.S. Lewis's *Screwtape Letters,* writes to his nephew Wormwood, in his usual contrary manner; "The humans live in time but our Enemy destines them to eternity. He therefore, I believe, wants them to attend chiefly to two things, to eternity itself, and to that point of time which they call the Present." [24]

Lewis goes on to explain, "This means that a continual looking forward to the eternal world is not (as some modern people think) a form of escapism or wishful thinking, but something a Christian should be doing. It does not mean that we are to leave the present world as it is. If you read history you will find that the Christians who did most for the present world were just those who thought most of the next. It is since Christians have largely ceased to think of the other world that they have become so ineffective in this. Aim at Heaven and you will get earth 'thrown in.' Aim at earth and you will get neither."

Jonathan Edwards explained the forceful resolution that determined his everyday decisions. "Resolved: To endeavor to obtain for myself as much happiness in the other world as I possibly can, with all the power, might, vigor and vehemence, yea violence, I am capable of, or can bring myself to exert, in any way that can be thought of." [25]

Pastor Erwin Lutzer says, "The person you are today will determine the rewards you will receive tomorrow. Those who are pleasing to Christ will be generously rewarded; those who are not pleasing to Him will receive negative consequences and a lesser reward. In other words, your life here will impact your life there forever." [26]

C.T. Studd, the great missionary, said, "Only one life, it will soon be past; only what's done for Christ will last." [27]

For all of these great men, the priority of the kingdom of God was the True North of their compass in life. It determined their decisions and the direction of their lives. They lived as they did because of their eternal destination.
Living in the light of eternity transforms the basis on which I make choices. I constantly ask myself, will what I am doing contribute to eternity?

DAY 6: QUESTIONS TO PONDER

What keeps you focused on the dot?

What keeps you focused on the line?

What are you doing today to impact your eternal tomorrow?

DAY 7: FOLLOWING JESUS

KEY VERSE

"And he said to all, "If anyone would come after me, let him deny himself and take up his cross daily and follow me. For whoever would save his life will lose it, but whoever loses his life for my sake will save it. For what does it profit a man if he gains the whole world and loses or forfeits himself?"

Luke 9:23-25

On July 4, 1952, a young English woman named Florence Chadwick waded into the water off Catalina Island intending to swim the channel to the California coast. Long distance swimming was not new to her: she was the first woman to swim the English Channel in both directions. But on this day, the water was numbingly cold, and a heavy fog rested over the water. She swam for fifteen hours before asking
to be taken out of the water by her team following along in boats. Her trainer urged her to keep going because she was close, only one mile from shore. But Florence just couldn't make it. "I'm not excusing myself, but if I could have seen the land, I might have made it." Two months later she did make it, because this time she could see her goal with every stroke.

My friend, if we are to achieve the goal of living in light of eternity, and do so over the long haul, then we are going to have to keep our eyes on the Lord Jesus Christ in a living daily relationship.

FOLLOWING JESUS

The whole process begins with a decision to take up the cross of Christ, because that is the route He took. We cannot avoid it. Three important words that describe Jesus' work on the cross also illustrate how we are to live as His followers. These three words are Salvation, Sacrifice, and Surrender.

The journey begins at the cross of Christ, the turning point of all history as well as your own life. The cross is not just behind us as the wonderful event that occurred at a specific point in time: the cross is also before us as we follow Jesus day by day. *"And he said to all, 'If anyone would come after me, let him deny himself and take up his cross daily and follow me'"* (Luke 9:23).
I remember a song I learned when I had just become a Christian at age 16. "I Have Decided to Follow Jesus" is a Christian hymn that originated in India. The lyrics are based on the last words of a man named Nokseng, in Garo, Assam, India. [28]

About 150 years ago, there was a great revival in Wales. As a result of this, many missionaries came to northeast India to
spread the gospel. The region known as Assam was home to hundreds of primitive, head-hunting tribes.
Into these hostile communities came a group of missionaries from the American Baptist Mission, spreading a message of love, peace, and hope in Jesus Christ. Naturally, they were not welcomed. One missionary succeeded in converting Nokseng, along with his wife and two children. This man's faith proved contagious, and many villagers began to accept Christianity.
Angry, the village chief summoned all the villagers. He then called this converted family to renounce their faith in public or face execution. Moved by the Holy Spirit, the man said: "I have decided to follow Jesus."
Enraged at the refusal of the man, the chief ordered his archers to arrow down the two children. As both boys lay twitching on the floor, the chief asked, "Will you deny your faith? You have lost both your children. You will lose your wife, too."
But the man replied: "Though no one joins me, still I will follow."

The chief was beside himself with fury and ordered his wife to be arrowed down. In a moment she joined her two children in death. Now he asked for the last time, "I will give you one more

opportunity to deny your faith and live." In the face of death, the man said the final memorable lines:
"The cross before me, the world behind me. No turning back."

He was shot dead like the rest of his family. But with their deaths, a miracle took place. The chief who had ordered the killings was moved by the faith of the man. He wondered, "Why should this man, his wife, and two children die for a man who lived in a far-away land on another continent some 2,000 years ago? There must be some remarkable power behind the family's faith, and I too want to taste that faith."
In a spontaneous confession of faith, he declared, "I too belong to Jesus Christ!" When the crowd heard this from the mouth of their chief, the whole village accepted Christ as their Lord and Savior. We tend to think that the world is before us and the cross behind us. Nothing could be further from the truth. The cross is before us and the world behind us!

SALVATION

 Managing money is not just a technical exercise of adding, subtracting, and calculating percentages and returns: it is essentially a spiritual discipline. We need to be set free from the power and influence money exerts over us. Jesus said, "No servant can serve two masters, for either he will hate the one and love the other, or he will be devoted to the one and despise the other. You cannot serve God and money" (Luke 16:13).

It is evident that money is powerful. So powerful that Jesus warns us that it competes against God for our allegiance and devotion. It has been said that we not only need to be taught how to use money but also to be constantly delivered from its power.
The cross of Christ offers us deliverance in three dimensions of time from three facets of sin: the penalty of sin, the power of sin, and ultimately, the presence of sin.

First, at the cross of Christ we have been delivered from the penalty of sin in our lives, becoming freely forgiven, free from all guilt and shame.

Second, due to the indwelling power of the Holy Spirit, we are daily being delivered from the power of sin over our lives. For the financial disciple this includes being saved from the power of money over our lives. We are to live in financial freedom: free from fear and anxiety, free from the burden of debt, free to love, free to serve, and free to enjoy all God gives us.

Last, we will become free from the presence of sin as we enter the promised land to be with Jesus in eternity, forever protected from evil.

The cross of Christ also reveals the true purpose of money in our lives. Money, when used for kingdom purposes, is just a means to a specific end – to help us and others grow in our intimacy with Christ. Do you understand that this is God's

purpose for money in your life? Remember, when we live with an eternal outlook, we embrace God's ownership of money: it all comes from God, it is all still God's, it is to be used for God, and the fruit from it is to go back to God. We are simply Christ's vessel in the equation – no more and no less.

SACRIFICE

Then Jesus said to them all, "If anyone would come after me, let him deny himself and take up his cross daily and follow me. For whoever would save his life will lose it, but whoever loses his life for my sake will save it. For what does it profit a man if he gains the whole world and loses or forfeits himself?" (Luke 9:23-25).

The words of the classic hymn by Isaac Watts [29] describe how the richest gains I have ever made in life pale into insignificance compared to the riches of the cross.

"When I survey the wondrous cross
On which the Prince of glory died, My richest gain I count but loss,
And pour contempt on all my pride.
Forbid it, Lord, that I should boast,
Save in the death of Christ my God:
All the vain things that charm me most, I sacrifice them to His blood.

Isaac Watts based this hymn on Galatians 6:14. "But God forbid that I should glory, save in the cross of our Lord Jesus Christ, by whom the world is crucified unto me, and I unto the world" (KJV). He sacrificed His life for us. We too are to live sacrificial lives, renouncing any rights we have to any property of our own. We are to give up our own desires and dreams and sacrifice all on the altar of the cross of Christ.
This is costly. The journey of discipleship, following Jesus, is not cheap or easy. Actually, inviting someone to follow Christ is like inviting someone to their own funeral – "I have been crucified with Christ …" (Galatians 2:20). My old life has been put to death, and new life "in Christ" has begun.

The cross in Jesus' day had one single purpose: to put someone to death. When calling us to become 'crucified with Christ,' Paul is not talking about giving things up for a cause. He is describing a complete abdication of all our rights, all our dreams and hopes. We are called to renounce, even out to death, all of our desires, our own agenda, our free time, our possessions and finances.

Sacrifice is a daily aspect of the life of a financial disciple. Paul gave us an urgent challenge. "I appeal to you therefore, brothers, by the mercies of God, to present your bodies as a living sacrifice, holy and acceptable to God, which is your spiritual worship." (Romans 12:1) According to Paul, we are not to live as the world lives and not to be conformed to its pattern of behavior. There is a compelling reason for the kind of sacrifice he is urging us to give. "Do not be conformed to this world, but be transformed by the renewal of your mind, that by testing you may discern what is the will of God, what is good and acceptable and perfect." (Romans 12:2)

John explains how Jesus set the standard for sacrifice. "By this we know love, that he laid down His life for us, and we ought to lay down our lives for the brothers." (1 John 3:16)life for us, and we ought to lay down our lives for the brothers."
There is a story about a pig and a chicken traveling together. The chicken gets hungry and sees a roadside restaurant. "Look, they

are serving bacon and eggs," said the chicken. "Let's go and have breakfast."
"No way," replied the pig. "For you it's a simple contribution, but for me it's total sacrifice!"
The chicken gets involved but the pig is totally committed!

I have to ask myself, Am I just involved with Jesus or totally committed to Him and His cause?

SURRENDER

 The most important example of surrender is Jesus Himself. Jesus completely surrendered to the will and to the plan of His Father. He gave up every single right He had as the Son of God, every entitlement. "Have this mind among yourselves, which is yours in Christ Jesus, who, though he was in the form of God, did not count equality with God a thing to be grasped, but emptied himself, by taking the form of a servant, being born in the likeness of men. And being found in human form, he humbled himself by becoming obedient to the point of death, even death on a cross" (Philippians 2:5-8). So are we to give up our lives, taking up our cross daily and following Him.

Charles Finney, a pivotal figure in American evangelism, was radical in this. In his "Lectures on Revival," he wrote in 1825,30 "Young converts should be taught that they have renounced the ownership of all their possessions and of themselves,
or if they have not done this, they are not Christians. They should not be left to think that anything is their own, their time, property, influence, faculties, bodies, or souls. The very idea
of being a Christian is to renounce self and become entirely consecrated to God. A man has no more right to withhold anything from God than he has to rob or steal. If God calls on them to employ anything they have, their money, or their time, or to give their children, or to dedicate themselves in advancing his kingdom, and they refuse because they want
to use them in their own way or prefer to do something else, it is vastly more blamable than for a clerk or an agent to go and

embezzle the money that is entrusted him by his employer, and spend it for his family or lay it out in bank stock or in speculation for himself."

Oswald Chambers, in his book My Utmost for His Highest, 31 notes: "The concept of 'surrender' [resignation] does not mean surrendering our external life, but our will. When that is done, there is nothing else to do. There are very few crises in life. The great crisis is the renouncing of your own will. It is very common today to listen to ministers invite people to make a 'commitment' to the Lord, instead of surrendering their lives to Christ."

A "commitment" is something I do for you, usually promising to do one thing in return for something else. Surrendering implies something quite different – giving myself over to you without reservation. If I surrender, I give you total control to do what you will with me. But in the twenty-first century, people don't want to surrender. They would rather live a version of the Christian life that retains control.

Hiroo Onoda, a Japanese soldier on the island of Lubang, in the Philippines, was isolated from his platoon and the rest of the world during World War 2. Despite countless efforts to inform him that the war was over, Onoda continued the fight for 29 years until finally, on March 10, 1974, he surrendered his rusty sword to the Philippine authorities, thus becoming the last Japanese soldier to surrender. Many of us take far too long to fully surrender to Christ. Surrender is not easy. But once we have invited Jesus into our lives, surrender to His authority is exactly what we need to end the internal war of our identity.

Christian leaders have long recognized the importance of this total surrender. Dwight L. Moody said, "The world has yet to see what can happen through a person fully surrendered to doing God's will." 32 Dawson Trotman, founder of the Navigators, added, "God can do more through one person who is 100 percent surrendered to Him, than through 99 who are only partially committed."

OBEDIENCE

In His 'Sermon on the Mount,' Jesus taught the foundational principles of the life of a disciple in the Kingdom of heaven. On finishing this teaching, Jesus closed by emphasizing the necessity not merely to hear what he was saying, but to obey and put it into practice.
"Everyone then who hears these words of mine and does them will be like a wise man who built his house on the rock. And the rain fell, and the floods came, and the
winds blew and beat on that house, but it did not fall, because it had been founded on the rock. And everyone who hears these words of mine and does not do them will be like a foolish man who built his house on the sand. And the rain fell, and the floods came, and the winds blew and beat against that house, and it fell, and great was the fall of it" (Matthew 7:24–27).

Jesus is saying that obedience to His words will give us a solid foundation on which to build our lives. Such a foundation will help us to overcome the storms of life. Not to obey His will is foolish because we will be left on a foundation of sinking sand, subject to all the forces of our environment.
Obedience to God's Word is the only way to build a foundation for life which will resist all the world can throw at us. In following Jesus day by day, I realize that any trials or troubles I have to go through are for a purpose: to prepare me for an eternity of co-working with Jesus.

When we take up the challenge to help others become financial disciples, we do well to follow the dedication of Ezra. During the rebuilding of Jerusalem under Nehemiah, he was responsible for taking the people back to the word of the Lord. *"For Ezra had set his heart to study the Law of the LORD, and to do it and to teach his statutes and rules in Israel"* (Ezra 7:10).
That is what we are supposed to do as financial disciples who help others find and follow Jesus: we learn, apply, and teach!

DAY 7: QUESTIONS TO PONDER

What does following Jesus look like for you?

Is God asking you to sacrifice something?

In what areas of your life is it hard to give up control?

What does obedience look like relative to financial discipleship?

PART 2: FINANCIAL FRUITFULNESS

DAY 8: FINANCIAL FRUITFULNESS

KEY VERSE

"But the fruit of the Spirit is love, joy, peace, patience, kindness, goodness, faithfulness, gentleness, self- control; against such things there is no law."

Galatians 5:22-23

Living a fruitful life is essential to growing as a financial disciple who qualifies to hear "Well done." This quality of life is produced only by the Holy Spirit in us. Being is more important than doing.

Before we examine financial specifics in Part 3 of this book, we first need to establish the qualities that the Master is looking for in our lives.

I would like to tell you a story about Zimmerman, a missionary to villages in Bosnia during the civil war in the early 1990s, when he meets Mihailovich, an old and influential man in the area.33 Mihailovich says, "How can I believe in a god who allows such horrible things to happen? The priests support the government; the church is stinking rich. I hate everything they stand for!" Zimmerman continued to visit the man for months and helped rebuild his damaged village. They also continued to debate faith in Jesus. The man's objections remained: he did not like the church. Zimmerman said one day, "Imagine, Mihailovich, that someone steals your coat and robs the bank. You run away, but someone has seen a man in your coat. The police maintain that it is you, and you are brought before them. What would you say?"

"Yes," said Mihailovich very deliberately, "I would say that someone else had put on the coat, and that the wrong person was in it." "Think about it," Zimmerman challenged him.

A few weeks later, Mihailovich told him, "I want to accept that Jesus. You wear his coat well!"

Jesus gave us a very important picture of a healthy financial disciple when He used the analogy of a vineyard in John 15. "Abide in me, and I in you. As the branch cannot bear fruit by itself, unless it abides in the vine, neither can you, unless you abide in me. I am the vine; you are the branches. Whoever abides in me and I in him, he it is that bears much fruit, for apart from me you can do nothing. If anyone does not abide in me he is thrown away like a branch and withers; and the branches are gathered, thrown into the fire, and burned. If you abide in me, and my words abide in you, ask whatever you wish, and it will be done for you. By this my Father is glorified, that you bear much fruit and so prove to be my disciples" (John 15:4-8).

FRUIT – THE MEASURE OF OUR SPIRITUAL HEALTH

 I wrote this during a great summer for fruit. A dry and hot summer is very advantageous for fruit growers, producing a bumper harvest and low prices for good, quality fruit. Love it!

The quality of a Christian's life is not his education, gifting, or talents – not even his Bible knowledge. It is the quality of his life's fruit. Jesus talked about a good tree bearing good fruit and a bad tree, bad fruit. *"You will recognize them by their fruits. Are grapes gathered from thornbushes, or figs from thistles? So, every healthy tree bears good fruit, but the diseased tree bears bad fruit"* (Matthew 7:16-17).

Fruit generally consists of three parts: stem, seeds, and flesh. The life from the tree flows through the stem, reproducing what is in the tree. So, if we are attached to the tree of life, which is Jesus Himself, we bring forth fruit that corresponds to His life. The fleshy part of the fruit is good to eat and sustains life, giving necessary nutrients to others. Then the fruit develops seeds that can be sown again to multiply the life of the tree.

I sometimes wonder what fruit I am bearing in my financial life.
Managing money well, in accordance with what God wants, can
be a tough struggle, but it doesn't need to be!
Being financially fruitful requires staying connected to the life of
Christ just as fruit stays connected to the tree. The dynamic life of
Christ will flow through our tree to bear good fruit. Being
financially fruitful means using our money for the good life
as we and others enjoy what our money can buy – just as we
would enjoy eating a juicy apple. This means sowing the seeds of
our money, investing in others and in the kingdom of God to
multiply what we have been given.

The apostle Paul described nine characteristics of spiritual life that
bring forth spiritual fruit, and this applies well to our money
management.
"The fruit of the Spirit is love, joy, peace, patience, kindness,
goodness, faithfulness, gentleness and self-control" (Galatians
5:22-23).

"Love" means using money to build meaningful relationships. *"Joy"*
is thanking God that He knows what I need and will provide all I
need. *"Peace"* is learning to be content in whatever circumstances
I find myself. *"Patience"* means to think twice before buying
something and to save slowly to build up assets. *"Kindness"* is
helping the poor and excelling in good deeds. *"Goodness"* is being
morally upright and honest in all my financial dealings.
"Faithfulness" is learning to use money in a way that honors God
and His purposes for my finances. *"Gentleness"* is humility and
meekness that is not boastful or proud. *"Self-control"* is being
disciplined in spending, saving, and giving.

When our fruit has these characteristics grown by the Spirit in us,
it tastes really good! Such fruit contains seeds that can be sown
into the lives of others to be multiplied and to grow again.
What really excites me is that fruit does not have to sweat or work
hard at all these things. All fruit needs to do is remain attached to
the right tree, accept the dynamic life coming out of the tree, and
allow itself to grow and be enjoyed. Being attached to the "Jesus

Tree" means to be diligent in study, fervent in prayer, and obedient to His leadership. Fruit from a "Jesus Tree" will almost automatically bear all these nine characteristics.

In contrast to this, fruit coming out of a "Me Tree" will not taste nice at all. Paul describes this as well. "Now the works of the flesh are evident: sexual immorality, impurity, sensuality, idolatry, sorcery, enmity, strife, jealousy, fits of anger, rivalries, dissensions, divisions, envy, drunkenness, orgies, and things like these. I warn you, as I warned you before, that those who do such things will not inherit the kingdom of God" (Galatians 5:19-21).

I really want people to recognize the fruit of the Spirit in my life so they get to experience something of who Jesus is by the quality of my life.

In the next nine Days we will look at how the life of Christ can work out His financial fruitfulness in your life. Enjoy the fruit!

DAY 8: QUESTIONS TO PONDER

How have you experienced financial fruitfulness?

Of the nine aspects of the Spirit's fruit (relative to financial fruit), which one resonates most with you? Which one seems the most challenging?

In what practical ways can I stay attached to a "Jesus Tree" to bear fruit?

Why is bearing the fruit of the Spirit so important in your financial discipleship journey?

DAY 8: LOVE

KEY VERSE

"So now faith, hope, and love abide, these three; but the greatest of these is love."

1 Corinthians 13:13

Well Done – Part 2: Financial Fruitfulness

Money is like love. It slowly and painfully destroys the one who withholds it and enriches those who use it for the good of their neighbor. Financial fruitfulness comes from using our money to love others. To love is to give. If you choose money over love, you will always be poor. We need to love people and use money instead of loving money and using people! Someone quipped, "you can use money to buy a dog, but only love will make it wag its tail!"

One Greek word for love is "*agape*," which carries the meaning of sacrificial giving, generosity that costs. We give, not out of any duty or compulsion, but because we love God. Giving is the logical reaction to the fact that God loved us first and gave us the most precious gift of all: salvation through the sacrifice of Jesus.
Agape love is more devotion than emotion: less feeling and more conscious choice. C.S. Lewis wrote, "Being in love is a good thing, but it is not the best thing . . . Love . . . is a deep unity maintained by the will and deliberately strengthened by habits reinforced by the grace which both partners ask and receive from God. On this love the engine of marriage is run; being in love was the explosion that started it."
Biblical love is a commitment to willingly sacrifice for the priority of God's work among the people He created and whom He loves – believers or not!

Are we using our money to love our neighbor as ourselves? Who is our neighbor? Jesus answered this question in the parable of the Good Samaritan. Our neighbor is one we come across in our daily life who needs help. The Samaritan took time out from his business, helped the one who had been attacked, took him to an inn, paid for his care, and even gave the hotelier a kind of "blank check" for whatever the man needed! He used his resources to demonstrate love. Love can be costly, but that should not discourage us: it is the very nature of God! (Read Luke 10:29-37).

During the many times I have spoken to people about money, one of the most recurring questions I get asked is about the biblical tithe. Should I give ten percent to the Lord's work? My answer is no. You should be giving one hundred percent to the Lord so that He can use any or all the resources under your management in any way He likes and as much as He likes.
Only when you have made the commitment to release to God all you control will you be in the right place to give at least ten percent to God's work in this world.
I ask people whom I teach, Who do you think was the most financially free person talked about in the New Testament? I think Jesus Himself told us when He described how a poor widow put two small copper coins into the offering in the Temple. *"She out of her poverty put in all she had to live on"* (see Luke 21:1-4). She gave all, not out of recklessness, but out of love for her God whom she was convinced would provide all she needed.

Love is a matter of the heart, which in a biblical sense is the center and seat of all spiritual life – the fountain of our thoughts, passions, and desires. Money has a strong connection to our heart, because our heart follows our money. Jesus said, "For where your treasure is, there your heart will be also" (Matthew 6:21). If we apply our money to God's work, then that's where our heart will be – with God. A very strong motivation to grow spiritually is to give to God's work: our heart follows our money!
If you want a heart for the lost, give to evangelistic movements. If you want a heart for the Church, support your local congregation financially. If you want a strong marriage, love your partner by

giving yourself and by planning and managing your finances, in prayer, together.

- The dimensions of love are described in 1 Corinthians 13:4-7. These have a lot to do with money.
- Love is patient. We can learn not to make impulsive buying decisions or enter into debt but rather wait and save for what we want to purchase.
- Love is kind. I can be generous and freely give my time, treasure, and talents.
- Love does not envy. I can be happy for what another has been able to buy as I am content and thankful for what I have.
- Love does not boast and is not arrogant. I can meditate on the fact that all I have in my possession has been given by God out of His grace, and not because of my own works.
- Love does not insist on its own way; it is not irritable or resentful. I can learn how to manage my money God's way. He is in control and gives me whatever I need – in His time. I can take wise advice, realizing I don't know it all!
- Love does not rejoice at wrongdoing but rejoices with the truth. I need to be honest and truthful in all my financial dealings and reporting.
- Love bears all things, believes all things, hopes all things, endures all things. When we believe we do not own anything but hold what we have in trust, then we can trust God and be thankful in any circumstances we find ourselves.

The Beatles sang, "money can't buy me love." True, but giving can make you rich. "One person gives freely, yet gains even more; another withholds unduly, but comes to poverty" (Proverbs 11:24, NIV).

Rich in God, rich in good deeds, rich in love!

Allowing the Spirit to produce love in me, out of love for the Lord I can serve people He brings across my path.

DAY 9: QUESTIONS TO PONDER

What is challenging about using money to help a "neighbor"?

How have you seen or experienced money being used to help a "neighbor"?

What areas of God's work do you have a heart for? How is this reflected in your finances?

How could expressing love help you on your financial discipleship journey?

DAY 10: JOY

KEY VERSE

"You make known to me the path of life; in your presence there is fullness of joy; at your right hand are pleasures forevermore."

Psalm 16:11

Don't worry, be happy!" This catchy song by Bobby McFerrin, released in the 1980s, still rings in our ears today. It suggests a simple remedy for troubling times, but we all realize it's just not that easy. Happiness as described by the Merriam- Webster dictionary is "an emotion evoked by well-being, success, or good fortune or by the prospect of possessing what one desires." The problem lies in the fact that life happens, circumstances change, problems crop up, and people don't do what we want them to do. Happiness is dependent on circumstances being right. Joy is different.

Theopedia describes it more convincingly as "a state of mind and an orientation of the heart. It is a settled state of contentment, confidence and hope." 34 This settled state of mind is that Biblical joy, which is not affected by external circumstances, but which chooses to be content, knowing that God can use any circumstance for His purposes in our lives.

One of the most challenging Christian concepts was described by Jesus' brother. "My brethren, count it all joy, when you fall into various trials, knowing that the testing of your faith produces patience" (James 1:2-3, NKJV).

These trials and the 'testing of our faith' can be endured because we know that the Lord has a purpose for why He allows them; in this verse from James, to develop patience, trusting Him.

Knowing that the Lord has a purpose for anything and everything we must endure, gives us a sense of joy because problems, trials and testing times yield positive benefits for the child of God. Trials and troubles are nu fun, but joy is something different.

If we need the strength to carry on, despite many trials and challenges, we need only to look to the Lord. ". . . the joy of the Lord is your strength" (Nehemiah 8:10).

Joy is not merely a euphoric feeling, arising out of pleasant circumstances. It comes because of choosing God's ways and understanding His purposes behind the circumstances. It helps me to remember that God is a master of recycling! He takes the

waste products of life and turning them into something useful.
That brings me great joy, deep inside!
The spiritual fruit called Joy enables us to be content and give
thanks in whatever economic circumstances we find ourselves.
Paul, writing not from the Ritz hotel but from
a Roman dungeon, understood this. "Rejoice in the Lord always. I
will say it again: Rejoice!" (Philippians 4:4, NIV). To Greek believers
he wrote, "Rejoice always, pray without ceasing, give thanks in all
circumstances; for this is the will of God in Christ Jesus for you. Do
not quench the Spirit"
(1 Thessalonians 5:16-19).

The Spirit of God in us produces this joy if only we will allow Him to
work in us. Henri Nouwen said, "Joy does not simply happen to us.
We have to choose joy and keep choosing it every day."

Today I read in the UK paper "Mail Online" this headline:
35"Generation who learned to count their blessings in Second
World War austerity are happier than their children." According to
research published in 2017, people living in 1957 were happier
than today. This found that although in 1957 life expectancies were
lower, Gross Domestic Product (GDP)
was lower, more hours were worked in a typical week, few
households had central heating, and less than half owned a
television, levels of public happiness were at a height never
reached again in the British postwar period. Researchers found no
connection between economic growth and the state of human
happiness in the long run.

Joy does not come from economic success. Joy does not come
from economic success. It springs from deep inside. It is a fountain
that never runs dry. Jesus is the fountain of gives such joy. He had
this joy in his heart, even under the shadow of the cross. "… And let
us run with perseverance the race marked out for us, fixing our
eyes on Jesus, the pioneer and perfecter of faith. For the joy set
before him He endured the cross, scorning its shame . . ." (Hebrews
12:1-2, NIV).

Perhaps it would be easier to describe where joy cannot be found:

- Not in unbelief – Voltaire was an unbeliever of the most pronounced type. He wrote: "I wish I had never been born."
- Not in pleasure – Lord Byron lived a life of pleasure if anyone did. He wrote: "The worm, the canker, and grief are mine alone."
- Not in money – Jay Gould, the American millionaire, had plenty of that. When dying, he said, "I suppose I am the most miserable man on earth."
- Not in position and fame – Lord Beaconsfield, prime-minister Benjamin Disraeli, enjoyed more than his share of both and came to the same conclusion as Solomon. He wrote: "Youth is a mistake; manhood a struggle; old age a regret."
- Not in military glory – Alexander the Great conquered the known world in his day. Having done so, he wept in his tent before saying, "There are no more worlds to conquer."

Where then is real joy found? The answer is simple: in Christ alone. Choose joy and allow the Spirit to flow, no matter your current economic conditions. It has little to do with the circumstances of our lives and everything to do with our focus.
Joy is a discipline that can be developed. Closely associated with self-control, the ninth characteristic of the fruit of the Spirit, joy is a byproduct of a life surrendered to the Spirit.

In his autobiography, Surprised by Joy, C. S. Lewis tells of experiencing an other-worldly joy – a specific joy that defies our modern understanding. This idea of joy is not a satisfied desire but an unsatisfied desire – a deep longing for God, a hungry pursuit of God's heart that never ends and is more satisfying than any earthly happiness.
Choosing joy in tough circumstances means to focus on God's purpose in trials and not on the problems themselves. "Count it all joy, my brothers, when you meet trials of various kinds, for you

know that the testing of your faith produces steadfastness. And let steadfastness have its full effect, that you may be perfect and complete, lacking in nothing" (James 1:2-4).

Choosing joy is to choose time in the presence of God, who will reveal His purposes to you. "You make known to me the path of life; in your presence there is fullness of joy; at your right hand are pleasures forevermore" (Psalm 16:11).
No matter what circumstances surround me, I will always choose to thank God, knowing He is in control – always. That brings me great joy!

DAY 10: QUESTIONS TO PONDER

What brings you the greatest joy?

How can you be joyful in the middle of trials?

What does it look like for you to choose joy on a daily basis?

DAY 11: PEACE

KEY VERSE

"You keep him in perfect peace whose mind is stayed on you, because he trusts in you. "

Isaiah 26:3

So, what does financial peace mean to you? For many, it means having a plan to control your expenses, not living from month to month, and having a savings account with enough set aside to meet emergency expenses. It means being free from debt and being able to meet mortgage payments or rent.

Well, these form the basic disciplines for financial peace, but this is not the spiritual financial fruit that the Holy Spirit produces in us. These disciplines have more to do with the ninth characteristic of the fruit of the Spirit, *"self-control."*

The apostle Paul wrote about the fruit of the Spirit in Galatians 5. We should note the meaning of the word "peace" in the Greek in which he wrote. *"Eirēne"* stems from *"eirō,"* meaning to join, to tie together into a whole – a wholeness in which all essential parts are joined together. Today, we would express *'eirene'* as "having it all together." Everything is in place and as it ought to be. Everything is complete., in its place and functioning as it ought to. In In Paul's days, people spoke a common Greek called *'koinone'* Greek.

"Eirene" was used in two ways. One was to denote the peace and quiet of a nation governed by a just and beneficent ruler.
 The other way was to describe a town or village, which had an official 'keeper of the public peace,' or keeper of the town's *'eirene.*

"Eirene" is the Greek equivalent to "shalom," which again means wholeness – all the parts working together in perfect harmony like a symphony orchestra. Picture many different instruments with different sounds played in different ways complementing one another to produce a beautiful piece of music that no single instrument could ever achieve.

The primary players that must be joined together to produce the financial fruitfulness of peace are God and myself. I can have exemplary self-control and discipline in my finances, enabling me to live off a well-defined financial plan, but if it is not God's plan, then I am missing "eirene" – God's peace. Ultimate peace is being reconciled to God and living in obedience to Him.
Very deliberately, Paul opens most of his letters to believers with the words "grace and peace." Grace must come before peace, and grace is a gift, an unmerited favor. Peace is given, not earned.
Jesus told his disciples, "Peace I leave with you; my peace I give you. I do not give to you as the world gives. Do not let your hearts be troubled and do not be afraid" (John 14:27, NIV).
So, are you constantly evaluating your financial life in the light of what God has to say about it? Are you following God's direction for your finances?

The next player in forming our symphony orchestra of financial peace is our marriage partner. *". . . A cord of three strands is not quickly broken"* (Ecclesiastes 4:12, NIV). Two conditions for financial peace in a marriage are regular communication and transparency. There is nothing wrong with husbands and wives earning their own money, keeping separate accounts, and having spending priorities; but all of these must be discussed and agreed upon in prayer with each other and with the
Lord. It is biblical that both accounts be considered together as one amount entrusted to them by the Lord. Arguments about money are a well-documented reason for marriage breakdown. Accepting Gods standards for financial peace will strengthen your relationship.

The final player in our symphony orchestra is our neighbor. One of the quickest ways to destroy trust is not paying what we have promised. Paying our bills on time builds trust; not meeting our obligations in full and on time brings unwanted "social distancing." The Bible is clear: *"The wicked borrows but does not pay back, but the righteous is generous and gives"* (Psalm 37:21). Financial peace requires loving your neighbor and giving what is due.

ENEMIES

 When I was a small boy growing up at the seaside, I loved to collect whelks and mussels. A whelk is a very small creature with an appendage that works like a small drill. It can bore a hole in the top of a shell, and through this very small hole suck out a mussel or even an oyster little by little until the whole thing has been devoured. Something very small like a whelk can destroy your financial peace.

The Greek philosopher Petrarch described the five great enemies of peace – greed, ambition, envy, anger, and pride – all having financial meanings.

What is stealing your financial peace?

Giving can act as an antidote to greed as you yield to the Spirit and act generously. Ambition can be overcome by accepting God's plan for your life. Envy can be defeated by learning contentment and thanking God for the success of others, rejoicing with them. Anger can be defeated through patience, understanding yourself, and putting yourself into the shoes of the one making you angry. The antidote to pride is humility, knowing yourself and your limitations.

I could easily add anxiety, which is very common in our economy today, to our list of enemies of peace. Worrying about money steals financial peace.

The most common questions I hear are, "Do I have enough?" and "Will I ever have enough?" Being able to determine "enough" for me and my family, with the responsibilities I have, will bring financial peace. Simply having more never satisfies: it only brings more to manage.

Anselm Grün is a Benedictine monk and a business manager. In his 2015 book, *Of Greed and Desire,* [36] he argues that the attitude of never having enough leads to a very unrestful behavior, "a nomadic existence" and "continual dissatisfaction." He writes, "When we desire possessions, we are looking for rest which we never find because we ultimately discover
that the possessions are possessing us and lead us into more needs."

Accepting *"grace and peace"* as a gift from our Lord will produce financial peace, no matter what the circumstances.
"You keep him in perfect peace whose mind is stayed on you, because he trusts in you. Trust in the LORD forever, for the LORD GOD is an everlasting rock" (Isaiah 26:3-4).

I gain a deep sense of peace when I trust the Lord to provide all I need to do all He is asking me to do.

DAY 11: QUESTIONS TO PONDER

What prevents you from having peace in your finances?

What could be possible antidotes to that lack of peace?

How could knowing the peace of God help you on your financial discipleship journey?

DAY 12: PATIENCE

KEY VERSE

"Wait for the LORD; be strong, and let your heart take courage;
wait for the LORD!"

Psalm 27:14

The fourth characteristic the fruit the Holy Spirit produces in our lives is patience. This is a very important aspect of financial fruitfulness. You get a chicken by slowly hatching an egg, not smashing it! Patience can be bitter – but the fruit is sweet.

Being patient is not easy in our modern culture. . Our culture says, "I want it, and I want it now!" We're constantly bombarded by messages trying to convince us to buy now, to spend now, to get what we want now. Patience, waiting for what we want is seldom practiced.

Amy Carmichael, missionary to India, wrote, "Blessed are the single-hearted, for they shall enjoy much peace. If you refuse to be hurried and pressed, if you stay your soul on God, nothing can keep you from that clearness of spirit which is life and peace. In that stillness you know what His will is." 37

I remember The Minority Report, a Spielberg movie starring Tom Cruise, which painted a disturbing picture of the future. One of its features was highly personalized advertising. Whenever you entered a shop, eye-retina scans would identify you. Every sign, every screen, and every sales placard would call you by name, show you all the products you have purchased or considered in the past, and showcase all the new, similar products in your preferred color, shape, and size. Sounded incredible at the time. Not now. Just log on to Amazon or Facebook, and the products you have previously browsed suddenly appear for you. Other products or people with a similar viewing history turn up too. And we are just at the beginning of big data influencing our lives and advising us what to buy.

DELAYED GRATIFICATION

Delayed or deferred gratification is resisting the temptation of an immediate pleasure in the hope of obtaining a valuable and longer-lasting reward. It means putting off buying what we want now in the hope that we can get something better later on. This essential discipline for financial fruitfulness requires the spiritual fruit of patience.

In a classic psychology experiment 38 from the 1970s, a psychologist named Walter Mischel placed a treat in front of children and offered them a choice. They could either enjoy the marshmallow now or wait a brief time in order to get two. When the experimenter left the room, many of the kids immediately ate the treat, but some were able to put off the urge to enjoy the treat now and wait for the reward of getting two delicious goodies later on. It is worthwhile to watch the short video "The Marshmallow Test," available on Youtube.

What Mischel discovered was that the kids who were able to delay gratification had a number of advantages later in life over the kids who simply could not wait. Years later, the children who had waited for the treat performed better academically than those who had eaten the treat right away. Those who delayed their gratification also displayed fewer behavioral problems and were much more successful in life.

The Holy Spirit can produce self-control in your life, which will enable you to forego something today in order to get something better in the future.

"The plans of the diligent lead surely to abundance, but everyone who is hasty comes only to poverty" (Proverbs 21:5). Having a plan and patiently working at it will lead to financial fruitfulness. Time is on our side because it stops us from making hasty decisions, allowing plans to mature and come to healthy fruition.

PATIENCE REVEALS OUR FAITH IN GOD

Patience shows that we trust God's timing, that he knows what he is doing and that He loves us. We generally look at 'being patient' as inactivity. The Greek word conveys more a sense of active trust. For example, Hebrews 12:1 says; "Therefore since we are surrounded by so great a cloud of witnesses, let us also lay aside every weight, and sin which clings so closely, and let us run with endurance the race that is set before us." The word 'patience,' is translated as 'endurance' which conveys strong sense of activity.

A Christian runs the race patiently by enduring tough times. In the Bible, patience is persevering toward a certain goal, continuing through trials in faith, waiting for God's promises to become reality. Being patient in our finances is realizing that money management is not a one-hundred-meter sprint, but more like a marathon. A "get rich quick" mentality leads to future loss. "Wealth gained hastily will dwindle, but whoever gathers little by little will increase it" (Proverbs 13:11).

Patience does not develop overnight, but gradually as you learn to trust and wait on the Lord. Colossians 1:11 tells us that we are, "being strengthened with all power, according to his glorious might, for all endurance and patience with joy." James tells us to, "count it all joy, my brothers, when you meet trials of various kinds, for you know that the testing of your faith produces steadfastness. And let steadfastness have its full effect, that you may be perfect and complete, lacking in nothing." (James 1:3,4)

BENEFITS OF PATIENCE

- Patience will help keep you out of debt as you learn to wait and save before making a major purchase.
- Patience will help you grow your money as you learn to save and then invest it.
- Patience teaches you discipline. I use the 30-day waiting list. Any major purchase goes on this list for prayer, further research for anything better, or an evaluation of whether I really need it.
- Patience allows you to seize future opportunities. If you are willing to save, you will be able to grasp hold of an outstanding opportunity when it appears.
- Patience helps you discover what's important. By nature, I am impulsive. But by waiting, I can evaluate if what I want to buy is really important when seeking the priorities of God's kingdom (see Matthew 6:33).

Leonardo DaVinci experienced ups and downs throughout his life When starting out in Florence, he was constantly ridiculed. He said, "Patience serves as a protection against wrongs as clothes do against cold. For if you put on more clothes as the cold increases, it will have no power to hurt you. So in like manner you must grow in patience when you meet with great wrongs, and they will then be powerless to vex your mind."

PATIENCE IS WAITING ON THE LORD

The Lord wants us to enjoy an abundant life, but this takes the fruit of the Spirit to make it possible. "I believe that I shall look upon the goodness of the LORD in the land of the living! Wait for the LORD; be strong, and let your heart take courage; wait for the LORD!" (Psalm 27:13-14).
Waiting on the Lord opens a door for His proactivity in my life. "From of old no one has heard or perceived by the ear, no eye has

seen a God besides you, who acts for those who wait for him"
(Isaiah 64:4).
I realize that waiting on the Lord for Him to act, in His time, in His
way is a strength, not a weakness. It will protect me from doing
things too quickly in my time and in my way!

DAY 12: QUESTIONS TO PONDER

What are the biggest challenges and roadblocks to delayed gratification in our world today?

How have you experienced the benefits of patience as it relates to your financial discipleship journey?

How could demonstrating patience help you on your financial discipleship journey?

DAY 13: KINDNESS

KEY VERSE

"Be kind to one another, tenderhearted, forgiving one another, as God in Christ forgave you."

Ephesians 4:32

Kindness is the fifth characteristic in the financial fruitfulness that gives evidence of the Holy Spirit's work in our lives.

In Middle English, the words "kind" and "kin" were the same. To show kindness is to become kin, family. Jesus' kindness to us was to become our "kin," our brother. When we demonstrate kindness, we become the family of the receiver; a kind of bond is created, a relationship begun.

I love Shakespeare's phrase, "the milk of human kindness." This is from a line by Lady Macbeth, complaining that her husband was not ruthless enough to become king. "Yet do I fear thy nature; it is too full o' the milk of human kindness to catch the nearest way." The source of "the milk of human kindness" is the very fact that we are all made in God's image; all acts of kindness stem from this. However, as one bishop said to another, "He has often heard of the milk of human kindness but never met the cow!" The effect of the milk is to nourish a healthy life. Kindness is as basic to our existence as milk is to a baby's growth.

Kindness is selfishly and willingly giving of your time, talent, and resources to improve the lives of others through acts of love and service. It is one of the most powerful forces for good. It is a practical way of expressing love. It is generosity in action.

The Holy Spirit produces kindness in us because it is an attribute of God Himself. "Or do you show contempt for the riches of his kindness, forbearance and patience, not realizing that God's kindness is intended to lead you to repentance?" (Romans 2:4, NIV).
Kindness is a choice, a choice to give away instead of keeping for yourself. There are so many tempting alternatives to kindness, – including doing nothing and selfishly putting our own interests first.

Circumstances can be testing; People trying; news troubling. But in the midst of testing, trials and troubles, we always have the opportunity to show kindness.

KINDNESS IN MARRIAGE

 Psychologist Dr. John Gottman studied thousands of couples to find out what makes marriage work. [139]The results of his study showed that lasting relationships come down to –
you guessed it – kindness and generosity. The lesson from the research is clear: If you want to have a stable, healthy relationship, exercise kindness early and often.

There are many reasons why relationships fail, but if you look at what drives the deterioration of many relationships, it's often a breakdown of kindness.

BIBLICAL EXAMPLE

 One of the most beautiful illustrations of the choice to be kind is King David's treatment of Mephibosheth in 2 Samuel 9. The chapter begins with David's question, "Is there not still someone of the house of Saul, that I may show the kindness of God to him?" (Verse 3).
David's wanted to demonstrate "the kindness of God" to King Saul's family because of his covenant with Saul's son, Jonathan.

The young man proposed to David was Mephibosheth, Jonathan's son, who was "crippled in his feet." David could easily have neglected Mephibosheth, who belonged to a condemned family. Instead, David was kind to Mephibosheth. He was terrified at appearing before the King. David assured him "Do not fear, for I will show you kindness for the sake of your father Jonathan, and I will restore to you all the land of Saul your father, and you shall eat at my table always" (verse 7).

BEING KIND

Kindness involves not just being disciplined and doing nice things but becoming kind – as a lifestyle.
Left to human nature, we would more readily show kindness to family and friends or to those from whom we want something. Biblical kindness produced by the Holy Spirit gives to those who cannot give in return, those who can do nothing for us but are in need of God's love.

Demonstrating kindness is keeping our eyes open for people in need and our spiritual hearts open to the prompting of
the Spirit to help someone and share our resources. Jesus gave us a great example of this, telling the story of the help a Samaritan traveler gave to an Israelite who had been attacked and left for dead beside the road. Kindness manifested itself in the Samaritan's awareness of people in need and his use of personal finances to help. After giving first aid, the Samaritan took the injured man to an inn. "And the next day he took out two denarii and gave them to the innkeeper, saying, 'Take care of him, and whatever more you spend, I will repay you when I come back'" (Luke 10:35).
Biblical kindness looks like Jesus, who gave all so that we could be free to become all we can be. As He lives His life through us, kindness becomes intentional, a habit, a lifestyle, a continual practice.

The Bible also says that kindness is a means God uses to overcome difficult times. The apostle Paul went through some really tough challenges. In 2 Corinthians 6:4-6, he notes "in afflictions, hardships, calamities, beatings, imprisonments, *riots, labors, sleepless nights, hunger . . ."* In all of this, he maintained that he could carry on serving people *"by purity, knowledge, patience, **kindness,** the Holy Spirit, genuine love"* (emphasis added). Kindness has a cost to it. It means giving to the other what we want to keep for ourselves. But that is love in action, sacrificial love, which fulfills the second of Jesus' great commandments: to love your neighbor as yourself. A great question to ask is, If I were in their shoes, what would I like them to do for me?

Kindness can change people's lives. Jack Canfield, in his encouraging book, *Chicken Soup for the Soul,* told about Mark Hansen, who was walking home from school one day when he noticed the boy ahead of him had tripped and dropped all of the books he was carrying – along with two sweaters, a baseball bat, a glove, and a small tape recorder. Mark knelt down and helped the boy pick up the scattered articles. Since they were going the same way, he helped to carry part of the burden. As they walked, Mark discovered the boy's name was Bill, that he loved video games, baseball, and history, that he was having a lot of trouble with his other subjects, and that he had just broken up with his girlfriend.

They arrived at Bill's home first, and Mark was invited in for a Coke and to watch some television. The afternoon passed pleasantly with a few laughs and some shared small talk,
and then Mark went home. They continued to see each other around school, having lunch together once or twice, and then both graduating from junior high. They ended up in the same high school, where they had brief contacts over the years.
Finally, the long-awaited senior year came. Three weeks before graduation, Bill asked Mark if they could talk.
Bill reminded him of the day years ago when they had first met. "Do you ever wonder why I was carrying so many things home that day?" asked Bill. "You see, I cleaned out my locker because I didn't want to leave a mess for anyone else. I had stored away some of my mother's sleeping pills and I was going home to commit

suicide. But after we spent some time together talking and laughing, I realized that if I had killed myself, I would have missed that time and so many others that might follow. So you see, Mark, when you picked up my books that day, you did a lot more. You saved my life." [40]

Paul commented on the kindness people in Philippi showed to him. *"I don't say this because I want a gift from you. Rather, I want you to receive a reward for your kindness"* (Philippians 4:17, NLT). Kindness is "paying it forward" and will not go unrewarded – now partially, but in eternity, fully!

DAY 13: QUESTIONS TO PONDER

How have you experienced someone's kindness improving your life?

How do you demonstrate kindness to others? What could the cost be?

How could demonstrating kindness help you on your financial discipleship journey?

DAY 14: GOODNESS

KEY VERSE

"In the same way, let your light shine before others, so that they may see your good works and give glory to your Father who is in heaven."

Matthew 5:16

Well Done – Part 2: Financial Fruitfulness

G oodness is the sixth characteristic in the financial fruitfulness that gives evidence of the Holy Spirit's work in our lives.

"And God saw everything that he had made, and behold, it was very good" (Genesis 1:31). During the creation, the Lord expressed his pleasure at the goodness of what He had
brought into being. The Hebrew word for this goodness is *"tov"*: this is anything that produces, sustains, and multiplies life. This is the purpose of creation and our purpose also – to bring forth goodness. God's fundamental goodness can create life from even the darkest of moments.
When our Jewish friends wish us well, they say, "Mazel tov!" In secular terms, it means "Good luck!" but the original meaning of *"mazzel"* is "dripping down." They are actually saying, "May the goodness of God drip down onto you."

The goodness of God can permeate our whole lives if we allow the Spirit to produce this in us. When I was a young boy, I grew up near the seaside town of Blackpool. I loved to eat what was called "a stick of rock," which was a hard candy with the word "Blackpool" all the way through it from top to bottom. No matter how I licked, the word was always there. Goodness is like that. No matter how much is "eaten," it still shows up!

The fruit is never used up. Goodness is an attribute of God's life in you and me.

When a rich, young leader came to Jesus to inquire about the conditions for eternal life, he addressed Jesus as "Good Teacher." Quite a normal way of addressing a respected teacher, you would say. Jesus replied, however, "Why do you call me good? No one is good except God alone" (Luke 18:19). Jesus immediately sets the standard for goodness. The rich, young ruler argued his worthiness by saying how well he had kept the commandments. He ran straight into a brick wall.

Proud of keeping some commandments, he failed to realize he had violated the second: "You shall have no other gods before me" (Exodus 20:3). In fact, mammon was his god, and money, his greatest problem.

The only way to live "good" is to allow the only One who is good to create this goodness in us through His Spirit. The Holy Spirit changes us from inside out and produces 'goodness' in us and help life to flourish. Goodness is not a quality we can develop on our own. James 1:17 says, "Every good thing given, and every perfect gift is from above, coming down from the Father of lights" (NASB).

When we allow the Holy Spirit to control us, we are blessed with the fruit of goodness. As others see our good works, they will praise our Father in heaven (see Matthew 5:16).

The Greek word Luke used to describe Jesus' word for "good," is the same word Paul used to describe this characteristic of the fruit of the Spirit: "agathos." This goodness is not merely a virtue of character but of actions that produce, sustain, and multiply life; it is for the benefit of others.

"Agathos" was not used in everyday Greek; it is a special term coined by believers as a way to express a kind of goodness that is deeper than anything the world experiences.

Here are four tests to see if my work is good, as in "tov" or "agathos."

"Agathos" work is prepared for us by God. "For we are his workmanship, created in Christ Jesus for good works, which God prepared beforehand, that we should walk in them" (Ephesians 2:10). For this reason, living out "goodness" always starts with prayer – asking God to show us which works He has prepared for us to carry out. These works will always reflect the uniqueness of our character and His purpose for our lives.

- Am I praying for God to reveal what He has prepared for me to do?
- Am I praying about which financial goals I should set and how I should allocate the money under my control

"Agathos" work is always excellent because it comes out of God's ability to work in us and through us. It is said of Jesus that the people "were astonished beyond measure, saying, 'He has done all things well'" (Mark 7:37).
- Does my work reflect God's excellence? Can people say of what I do, "Well done, that's great!"?
- Is my financial administration in good order?

Agathos" work has the right motive: to serve God first and foremost and then to love our neighbor.
- Do I make my decisions out of love for God and the people around me?
- Do I choose God and people above financial goals?

"Agathos" work is productive. This means to use the resources I have been given to produce something people find useful for themselves.
- Does my work help people, including my employer or customers, to effectively achieve their goals?
- Am I using money to help people flourish?

I realize that only God is good, and that any goodness coming out of my life is generated from the Father Himself as I open myself to the Spirit's leadership.

DAY 14: QUESTIONS TO PONDER

The "Agathos" Test:
- Are you praying for God to reveal what He has prepared for you to do?

- Are you praying about which financial goals you should set and how you should allocate the money under your control?

- Does your work reflect God's excellence? Can people say of what you do, "Well done, that's great!"?

- Is your financial administration in good order?

- Do you make decisions out of love for God and the people around you?

- Do you choose God and people above financial goals?

- Does your work help people, including your employer or customers, to effectively achieve their goals?

- Are you using money to help people flourish?

DAY 15: FAITHFULNESS

KEY VERSE

"If then you have not been faithful in the unrighteous wealth, who will entrust to you the true riches? And if you have not been faithful in that which is another's, who will give you that which is your own?"

Luke 16:11-12

Faithfulness is the seventh characteristic in the financial fruitfulness that gives evidence of the Holy Spirit's work in our lives.

I fondly remember traveling with an ex-marine through the Scandinavian nations on a mission to share the gospel with business people. Ralph Spencer began every day by saying, "Another day to excel, another day to the glory of God. Semper fi." Semper fi is the motto of the US marines, meaning "always faithful."Faithful people seem hard to find, according to King Solomon. "Most men will proclaim every one his own goodness: but a faithful man who can find?" (Proverbs 20:6, KJV). So, faithfulness among people is scarce, but not so with God.

The biblical word for faithful is *"pistis"* which is considered to be one of God's personal characteristics. He is a maker of promises, which He always keeps – even when we don't!
"Pistos" is used in secular Greek for trustworthy, dependable, loyal. It is used to describe people who show themselves faithful in business transactions or in the discharge of official duties. That kind of man or woman is worthy of trust and can be relied on.

Jesus told of three people who had to give account after receiving one, two, and five talents respectively to manage (see Matthew

25:14-30). One talent was about six-thousand silver drachmas, and one drachma was an average daily wage. Quite a lot! For the two stewards who understood what they had to do and went to work using the master's money, there was a nice reward. *"Well done, good and faithful servant. You have been faithful over a little; I will set you over much. Enter* into the joy of your master." The reward for good stewardship was more responsibility! He could be trusted with more because he had been faithful with little. More responsibility, more to manage, and better yet – the joy of his master!
But the one who had received one talent was scared and lazy, despising the trust given to him by the master. He was severely sentenced.

I have asked many people what they would like to hear once they have come to our Lord Jesus Christ. I almost unanimously hear "Well done good and faithful servant." They want to know that Jesus is pleased with the life they led and how they managed what He entrusted to them. The Bible shows us in the parables of the kingdom that faithful stewards who use and multiply the master's resources can expect to be partially rewarded in this life – and in the next one, fully rewarded.

We talk a lot about trusting God, but I think the harder, reflective question is: Can God trust me?
After telling a story (Luke 16:1-9) of a manager about to be fired after being accused of wasting his master's possessions, Jesus followed up with three lessons in financial faithfulness in verses 10-12. In these, He gave His followers three areas in which they were to be financially faithful. "One who is faithful in a very little is also faithful in much, and one who is dishonest in a very little is also dishonest in much. If then you have not been faithful in the unrighteous wealth, who will entrust to you the true riches? And if you have not been faithful in that which is another's, who will give you that which is your own?"

He gives us three word pairs that help us use money without being used by it. The three word pairs are: "Little/much," "false/

real," and "another's/ours."

Faithfulness in little things is the supreme standard to which a good manager should adhere. It is a prerequisite to be trusted with much! When giving assignments, either as a parent with our children or as or a manager with our employees, we evaluate what they do with small tasks; if we find that they have been faithful with those, we know we can go on to trust them with more responsibility. Dishonesty in what we may consider small things, like cheating on expenses or taxes, has consequences in the extent to which God can trust us.

Secondly, faithfulness in "unrighteous wealth" is a prerequisite for what Jesus called "true riches." Money is not just paper or coin: it is subject to a power that Jesus unmasked and called "mammon." This power is in itself unrighteous and will compete for our devotion. In verse 13, Jesus warns us that we cannot serve both God and money. We have to learn to manage this power. We begin by realizing that it is a defeated power through Jesus. Then we prayerfully learn to use money God's way. If we are faithful in using our money God's way, then Jesus says He can trust us with *"true riches."* I believe this to mean a very intimate relationship with God, experiencing all He wants to trust us with, both now and eternally.
Lastly, we are to be faithful in *"that which is another's,"* before God can trust us with money and possessions of our own.

The Bible teaches clearly that all belongs to God – we do not own anything. We are raised to think that we are the owners of everything we have worked for and earned. The business belongs to me, my house, my car, my money. Jesus says, "No, it belongs to another!" In fact, we own nothing: we only have it to manage and utilize. God's ownership means that we have access to use.
What does this look like for you in everyday life? Do you really live out this perspective each day?

Realizing that God owns everything, we can have access to all He has to give – if only we are faithful in using what he has already entrusted to us, be it much or little.

Paul wrote in 1 Corinthians 4:1-4, "This is how one should regard us, as servants of Christ and stewards of the mysteries of God. Moreover, it is required of stewards that they be found faithful. But with me it is a very small thing that I should be judged by you or by any human court. In fact, I do not even judge myself. For I am not aware of anything against myself, but I am not thereby acquitted. It is the Lord who judges me."

Paul realized that it was his responsibility to be faithful but also that he could not accomplish this on his own. It is Jesus who will determine whether we are faithful!

The late US senator Mark Hatfield tells of touring Calcutta with Mother Teresa and visiting the so-called "House of Dying," where sick children are cared for in their last days. He also toured the dispensary, where the poor line up by the hundreds to receive medical attention. Watching Mother Teresa minister to these people, feeding and nursing those left by others to die, Hatfield was overwhelmed by the sheer magnitude of the suffering she and her co-workers faced daily. "How can you bear the load without being crushed by it?" he asked. Mother Teresa replied, "My dear Senator, I am not called to be successful; I am called to be *faithful*." [41]

DAY 15: QUESTIONS TO PONDER

How would you describe yourself as it relates to: Being faithful in the little things?

Being faithful with unrighteous wealth?

Being faithful with "that which is another's"?

How could being faithful help you on your financial discipleship journey?

DAY 16: GENTLENESS

KEY VERSE

"Take my yoke upon you, and learn from me, for I am gentle and lowly in heart, and you will find rest for your souls."

Matthew 11:29

Gentleness is the eighth characteristic in the financial fruitfulness that gives evidence of the Holy Spirit's work in our lives. The word the New Testament uses for gentleness is *"prautes."* This word is derived from "praus," the Greek word for meekness, which can be described as "gentle strength."

Charles Swindoll writes, "In our rough and rugged individualism, we think of gentleness as weakness – being soft and virtually spineless. Not so. Gentleness includes such enviable qualities as having strength under control, being calm and peaceful when surrounded by a heated atmosphere, emitting a soothing effect on those who may be angry or otherwise beside themselves, and possessing tact and gracious courtesy that causes others to retain their self-esteem and dignity. Instead of losing, the gentle gain; instead of being ripped off and taken advantage of, they come out ahead." [42]

We have been granted access to the power of the Holy Spirit which produces in us the fruit of gentleness. Being gentle or meek (the Greek *'prautes'*) recognizes that we are not the source of this power but the means by which this power is expressed. Gentleness is not the relinquishing of this power but bringing it under the authority of the Father. John the Baptist seemed to understand this well when he said, "He must increase, but I must decrease." (John 3:30)

It is the opposite of arrogance, which is the unholy trinity of "me, myself, and I" exercising power independently and selfishly. Vine's Expository Dictionary defines "prautes" as an attitude toward God, submitting oneself to God, not resisting God, confident in God's presence, authority, and power. "Prautes" gives calmness of spirit from a mental focus that is not on self or prioritizing personal desires. "Prautes" seeks and wants what the Creator of life desires. "Prautes" is being confident that God is in charge – and accepting it.

This Greek word can be read in classical literature to describe a horse that someone had broken and trained to take be bridled and saddled. It paints a picture of strength under control. In our case, strength under control of the Holy Spirit, as we place ourselves under the authority of God's Word.
A friend of mine lives in Belfast and keeps donkeys as a hobby. Sometimes he earns money by taking in a young, aggressive, thoroughbred racehorse that is tough to handle. He has a wonderful way of taming the horse. He brings the horse into the stable with a donkey and ties the bit in the horse's mouth with a short rope to the donkey. He leaves them overnight, and the next morning, the horse is as tame as a lamb! The donkey is so stubborn and strong-willed that he will not allow the horse to move around. The horse's will is broken.

Our own stubborn, prideful, independent will is broken by getting into close connection with Jesus and responding to his wonderful invitation, "Come to me, all who labor and are heavy laden, and I will give you rest. Take my yoke upon you, and learn from me, for I am gentle and lowly in heart, and you will find rest for your souls. For my yoke is easy, and my burden is light" (Matthew 11:28-30). We can be harnessed to Jesus with a yoke that, in contrast to an oxen yoke, is light and easy. Jesus produces in us this fruit of the Spirit of gentleness.

This meekness is the unassuming inner spirit of mildness and gentleness, the opposite of haughtiness, harshness, and self-

assertiveness. Jesus placed Himself completely under the control of His Father, setting aside all rights.
Meekness can only exist where strength is strictly under control. It describes a domesticated animal that has been carefully trained for its master's purposes – even the taming of wild animals. Meekness is "strength under control," clearly demonstrated by Jesus.
Weakness and meekness are not synonyms. Weakness says, "I can't." Meekness says, "I can!" It acknowledges God's control and authority over a given situation.

When demonstrating meekness, we accept is seeing everything as coming from God and accept it without complaining, waiting patiently, and submitting, as Jesus did, to any and every wrong we may suffer with without any desire for revenge or retribution. Financial fruitfulness comes from submitting ourselves completely to the Lord and following biblical principles for managing our money and possessions. We need to stay close to Jesus and take His yoke on us. If we are in a yoke with Jesus, and submissively follow the direction He wants to take us, He promises us financial peace and inner rest.

If one ox in a yoke with another does not stay at an equal pace with the other, it could easily break its back. Partners in a yoke must follow the same direction and pull together. The yoke of Christ for us is His mission, "to serve" (Mark 10:45) and "to set the oppressed free" (Luke 4:18, NIV). Being in a yoke with Jesus inevitably takes you to the cross. People who are meek have been to the cross and understand what Jesus meant by "take up your cross daily and follow me" (Luke 9:23, NLT). Meekness says, "I renounce all in order to gain all."

Managing our finances is a partnership with God. He has a part to play, and I have a part to play. I can never, ever do what only He can do. And He will not do what I must do! Do you look at managing your finances as a partnership with God or as a sole proprietorship where you do as you wish?

His part? To provide what we need, to give us direction, and to impart wisdom on how to use resources well. My part? To learn His direction, to faithfully implement biblical principles, to be generous at His bidding, to serve others, and to enjoy all He gives me. You can't manage your finances God's way
without humility, submitting to the leadership of the Spirit, and obeying biblical instruction.
The financial fruit of gentleness, or meekness, is allowing the power of God Himself to flow through our lives to His glory and the benefit of others. Then in every situation, whether having plenty or being in need, we can cry aloud, together with Paul *"I can do all things through him who strengthens me"* (Philippians 4:13).

I never thought about gentleness as a strength; it's not something men naturally think about. Strength, yes, but I realize this is controlled power, through the Spirit.
Gentleness or meekness is power under control, which leads us directly to the next topic: self-control.

DAY 16: QUESTIONS TO PONDER

In what ways can gentleness be a strength in your life?

If we know that Jesus' yoke is light and easy, what stops us from taking that yoke?

What would Jesus' light and easy yoke look like as it relates to your financial discipleship journey?

DAY 17: SELF-CONTROL

KEY VERSE

"A man without self-control is like a city broken into and left without walls."

Proverbs 25:28

Well Done – Part 2: Financial Fruitfulness

The final characteristic of the fruit that the Holy Spirit produces in our lives is self-control. The wise King Solomon wrote the proverb above as a useful illustration of our need for self-control.

In his time, a city depended on strong fortifications with great walls surrounding it to repel ravaging bands of guerrillas or foreign armies. If the gates or towers or walls were broken down, a city was totally exposed to any enemy that wished to plunder, pillage, or conquer it. If a city did not invest sufficiently in its protection, it could easily be captured. A man without the power to rule his spirit is just as exposed and vulnerable as a defenseless city.

Our own experience shows us that we are not capable, in ourselves, of controlling ourselves. Even the great apostle Paul honestly admitted, *"For I know that nothing good dwells in me, that is, in my flesh. For I have the desire to do what is right, but not the ability to carry it out. For I do not do the good I want, but the evil I do not want is what I keep on doing"* (Romans 7:18-19). That's why self-control is a fruit of the Spirit and not the result of our own power of discipline.

The philosopher and statesman Edmund Burke wrote, "Men are qualified for civil liberty in exact proportion to their disposition to put moral chains upon their own appetites … Society cannot exist, unless a controlling power upon will and appetite be placed somewhere." [43]

That controlling power is the Holy Spirit, who gives us the power to do that which we cannot do ourselves. Self-control is like wanting to lift ourselves off the ground using our own boot laces. We cannot do that; we need a power outside of ourselves to control our lives.

In contrast to his proverb quoted above, Solomon said, "Whoever is slow to anger is better than the mighty, and he who rules his spirit than he who takes a city" (Proverbs 16:32).
The great King Solomon accomplished much but did not finish well because of the absence of self-control in his life. He was intelligent and knew what to do but could not control his passions. He did not heed the conditions God placed on kingship. *"And he shall not acquire many wives for himself, lest his heart turn away, nor shall he acquire for himself excessive silver and gold"* (Deuteronomy 17:17). As we know, in the end he failed miserably!

The Spirit will produce in us the power to say no, the ability to carry out our promises, and the means by which we can control our desires, subjecting them to the will of God. On the positive side, the Spirit will help us to control our talents, skills, and gifting so that we can build wealth. *"You shall remember the LORD your God, for it is he who gives you power to get wealth . . ."* (Deuteronomy 8:18).

What are the "walls" of the "city" of my financial life? The wall around financial fruitfulness is formed by living within your harvest. This means learning to live on what comes in and being content with it. Living within your harvest is possible – but it is surely counter-cultural. It acknowledges that we have accepted some limitations and that we are willing to confine ourselves within the scope of these boundaries rather than pine for the proverbial greener grass on the other side of the fence.
Contentment and simplicity help us in this effort to live within limits. Be content with what God sends your way and learn to live

a simple life. This honors God and we allow Him to tend to our harvest

THE SPENDING PLAN

 Practically, this means setting up a spending plan to manage the resources at our disposal. Such a plan can be pictured as a pie with three main segments.

First, list the fixed expenses that are relatively constant each month. This would include your tithe, mortgage or rent payments, insurance, local taxes, subscriptions, transportation, and energy bills. Then, figure out how much you will need for a buffer and for important future goals and purchases. Subtract these two amounts from your income and divide by four. That is how much you have left to live on each week.

Such a plan should be set up together with God in prayer. When we have this complete, it is like saying, "Lord, if you will provide what we have just agreed on, then that will be enough for me – for all my responsibilities and to do all you are asking me to do. I thank you, in advance, for your provision, and I
will be content with what you give me. If you should give me more, I will not spend it on myself and allow the "pie" to get bigger, but I will use the excess to bless my family and extend your kingdom."
If I do not have a spending plan, a budget, and if I cannot say "this is enough," then I open myself up to all kinds of temptations to keep on spending. Outside inducements such as advertising and peer pressure as well as the inside temptations of greed and emotional insecurity will lead us to spend more on our lifestyle – which is ever expanding and needs ever-increasing financing! We need to say no to these voices of the world's system that constantly tempt us to increase our spending. If I give into the world's standards, I will not be able to fulfill God's purpose for my life – to reach my life goals, be generous, and most importantly, glorify Him in all I do!
Professor Dr. Tomas Sedlacek, in his book *The Economics of Good and Evil* wrote, "The more we have, the more we want. Why?

Perhaps we thought that the more we have, the less we will need. We thought that consumption leads to saturation
of our needs. But the opposite has proven to be true. The more we have, the more additional things we need. Every new satisfied want will beget a new one and will leave us wanting. For consumption is like a drug."[44]
Answering the question, How much is enough? leads to peace, rest, satisfaction, and contentment. The answer lies in a spending plan that allows us to live within our harvest. Spend less than you earn over a long period of time, and you will be able to build wealth that enables you to love God and those close to you.

DAY 17: QUESTIONS TO PONDER

What are the "walls" of the "city" in your financial discipleship journey?

If you don't have a spending plan, what is hindering you from using one?

How could demonstrating self-control help you on your financial discipleship journey?

PART 3: MULTIPLYING YOUR RESOURCES

DAY 18: BUILDING WEALTH

KEY VERSE

"You shall remember the LORD your God, for it is he who gives you power to get wealth, that he may
confirm his covenant that he swore to your fathers, as it is this day."

Deuteronomy 8:18

Wealth is an abundance of resources we can use. The purpose of building wealth in all its dimensions is to fully participate in the life God has given us, to take care of and enjoy His creation, and to be a blessing to those He brings across our path.

Henry David Thoreau said, "Wealth is the ability to fully experience life." We agree and add one huge qualifier: In our case, it includes eternal life!

God promises us the ability to multiply our resources. Early on He promised that obedience to His commandments and rules would make the children of Israel wealthy. "Take care lest you forget the LORD your God by not keeping his commandments and his rules and his statutes, which I command you today, lest, when you have eaten and are full and have built good houses and live in them, and when your herds and flocks multiply and your silver and gold is multiplied and all that you have is multiplied, then your heart be lifted up, and you forget the LORD your God, who brought you out of the land of Egypt, out of the house of slavery" (Deuteronomy 8:11-14).

Above all, during all this prosperity, they were not to forget the source of their wealth. "Beware lest you say in your heart, 'My power and the might of my hand have gotten me this wealth.' You shall remember the LORD your God, for it is he who gives you power to get wealth, that he may confirm his covenant that he swore to your fathers, as it is this day" (Deuteronomy 8:17-18). Building wealth in God's economy starts with God's provision. When Moses was leading the people of Israel into the promised land, he warned them not to forget God, who brought them out of slavery, out of the land of "not enough," through the desert of "just enough" and into the land of "more than enough." Abundance is promised. Unfortunately, a lot of Christians are living in the land of "just enough" and have not traveled further.

THE PURPOSE OF WEALTH

When Moses wrote in Deuteronomy 8:18 that God gives power to create wealth, the Hebrew word used for wealth is *"haiyl,"* which is most often used in the Bible to mean an army of people. It seems as though God's priority is for wealth to be used to invest in the prosperity of people, to make them healthy, productive, in harmony with one another, and able to enjoy all God's gifts.
The purpose of being given the power to create wealth is stated in Deuteronomy 8:18, *"that he may confirm his covenant that he swore to your fathers, as it is this day."*
So, what is this covenant?

This is the covenant of Abraham, described in Genesis 12:2. God promises, "I will make of you a great nation, and I will bless you and make your name great, so that you will be a blessing."
Five times in Genesis 12 as God is giving the covenant to Abraham, He says, *"I will."* Clearly, God is taking upon Himself the responsibility for keeping the covenant.

The covenant promised to build up a nation of people to be blessed by God and to be given a land in which to enjoy these blessings. It promised many descendants – even from a childless, old couple! God repeated the covenant to Isaac and to his son Jacob, whose name God changes to Israel. The great nation is eventually established in the land where Abraham had dwelled. A further covenant was given to King David, one of Abraham's many descendants. This promised a royal line out of

David, which will eventually reach its fulfillment with the "Son of David", the messiah who will rule the renewed world out of Jerusalem. (2 Samuel 7:12–16)

The covenant between God and Abraham also established a land to be occupied, one *"flowing with milk and honey,"* a land of abundance.
This covenant has now been superseded for us with the new covenant in Jesus. The promises to Abraham of many descendants and a land of abundance are now ours. For the time being, we are *"strangers and aliens"* on this earth, waiting for that time when we can fully enter the promised land of eternity – the new earth.
The Lord is gathering a nation of people from "every tribe and language and people and nation" (Revelation 5:9). The Lord's part is to call and gather people; our part is to go in the authority and power of Christ to make disciples in all nations (see Matthew 28:19-20).
We are given the opportunity to contribute to this new nation of redeemed people as Jesus gives us the ability to be *"fishers of men"* (Matthew 4:19).

THE FIVE FORMS OF WEALTH

 The term we will use for true personal wealth is life wealth, or wealth. This can be defined as follows:
Life wealth is the accumulation of financial, relational, physical, productive, and spiritual wealth, with which God can realize His goals through us.
The definition above uses the term "wealth," which refers to the assets or resources we can develop to accumulate life wealth and then use to reach our goals. Wealth is normally used for a sum of money used in business. However, life wealth does not come only from money. In addition to financial wealth are four other very important forms of life wealth: spiritual wealth, physical wealth, relational wealth, and productive wealth.

1.   **Financial wealth** is the money and possessions we have to spend, give, and invest. We start with this one, not because it is the most important but because it is the most obvious, the easiest to identify and measure.
When we think financial wealth is most important, we become willing to sacrifice other kinds of wealth to get it. I remember sacrificing the more important types of wealth in my attempt to maximize financial wealth. I worked many hours at the office to earn a large salary, with the unintended consequence of sacrificing relational wealth with my children. They wanted me home to read a story and tuck them in at night. And with my wife, who wanted more time together. I also sacrificed my physical wealth, working so much that my health began to fail. I sacrificed spiritual wealth because I neglected my relationship with Jesus for a long time. Eventually, my life stopped working properly because I'd made a foolish investment, sacrificing wealth that was more valuable (spiritual, relational, physical) to grow wealth that was less valuable (financial).

To build our financial wealth, we should be investing – not neglecting – our other forms of wealth.
Invest spiritual wealth by studying what the Bible has to say about managing money – God's way! The Lord will give you guidance and strength to make the right plans and stick to them.

Invest relational wealth by asking a friend to keep you accountable for staying within your budget. Ask friends or more experienced people in your life for advice on your financial planning process. Invest productive wealth in researching best buys, saving money, reading about financial planning, and developing your talents and skills to earn money.
Invest physical wealth by actively protecting your body's health (this includes your brain) through diet, exercise, and study.

2. **Physical wealth** is the health and energy strength we have available to invest. This directly impacts how effective we can be in

carrying out tasks, projects we have to do. If we are not healthy, we cannot enjoy our most meaningful relationships as much as we would like. We need to find a good balance between work and rest to enable us to work hard and efficiently. Jesus teaches His disciples to come to Him, rest and abide in Him so that we can live fruitful lives. (see Matthew 11:28-30 and John 15:5).. Central to investing in physical wealth is simply honoring the limitations we have as humans.

Should physical wealth be ranked higher than productive and financial wealth? If we're sick, we can't work (financial and productive wealth). Likewise, if we have a migraine, we can't deliver a lecture or write a book (productive wealth). We can't solve a problem in a brainstorming meeting if we're home ill. No amount of money or ideas can replace the value of being physically present, giving time and attention to people or projects. It's fascinating how interdependent these wealths are. To build our physical wealth, we can invest the other four forms of wealth. For example, one way to grow our physical wealth is simply to take a day off once a week. Taking a day off is a way of investing financial wealth to grow physical wealth, since we are sacrificing a day of making money in order to rest. We can set aside the urge to produce and simply focus on resting, recreating, and enjoying life one day per week. The Lord gave us an example of resting on the seventh day after creation and gave us a command to follow His lead. When we do this with our family, we grow our physical and relational wealth together!

Another way to grow our physical wealth is to get healthier. Better health allows us to be better stewards of our time, because we have more energy for the tasks of the day and more mental clarity for problem solving. And we don't get sick as much. Healthy people just get more done.
To grow our physical wealth, we might want to get a gym membership (investing financial wealth). We might read a few books on eating better (investing productive wealth). We might want to ask a friend to join us at the gym for some accountability (investing relational wealth). We might also

make it a matter of prayer and study, looking at what Scripture says about the healthy rhythm of work and rest (investing spiritual wealth).

3. **Relational wealth** is measured by the quantity and quality of our relationships. We have friends, family, and co-workers to help us achieve what we want out of life.
In the gospels, we can read how Jesus invested His physical wealth to grow relational wealth – His disciples. This was smart, because teaching thousands of people, expecting them to carry on His mission is much more difficult and uncertain than training a small number of disciples intensively. He built His relational wealth so that the disciples, in turn, could follow His examples and do the same with others. The multiplication began.
Relational wealth is more valuable than physical, productive, and financial wealth, because we can't do anything of value in life without a relationship of mutual trust. Without relational wealth we are essentially islands, living to ourselves. In that state, how can we do anything meaningful with our physical, productive, or financial wealth?

In the Gospels, we see Jesus consistently investing relational wealth and training His disciples to do the same. Once He chose twelve of his disciples to be designated "apostles,"
He prioritized His time and investment in those twelve, developing deep relational wealth with them as He trained them. We also see Him repeatedly returning to the home of Mary, Martha, and Lazarus in Bethany, cultivating relational wealth with them and using their home as both a retreat and a base of operations.
Jesus encourages us to *"use worldly wealth to make friends,"* so it's not a bad idea to set some money aside to take people out or have them over for dinner once a week (investing financial wealth). Investing productive wealth could look like helping people with things you know how to do and sharing your expertise with others. Someone is always in need of help with a car, a computer, a phone, whatever your skill or hobby might entail. Spending time with people (investing physical wealth) is an indispensable part of any relationship.

You'll also want to invest your spiritual wealth by praying for those with whom you want to grow in relational wealth. Ask God to give you a word of encouragement for them

4. Productive wealth is is the know-how, wisdom, creativity, and knowledge we have available to invest. It is formed by the gifts, talents, and natural abilities with which we have been endowed. Jesus possessed an amazing level of productive wealth, which He used often in His mission. In the culture of His day,
He was accepted by people He met as a 'Rabbi," which is a teacher or master. Dallas Willard quipped, "Jesus wasn't just nice, he was brilliant!"
People were amazed by the quality of His ministry. "And they were astonished beyond measure, saying, 'He has done all things well." (Mark 7:37).
Productive wealth is built up through learning and training.

Benjamin Franklin said, "An investment in knowledge pays the best interest."
It is worth spending other types of wealth, like financial and relational to get productive wealth.
When we think of productive wealth, we think mainly about know-how, but it is the ability to make good use of this know-how in a timely manner that makes the knowledge useful. A CEO of a large company said, "Customers will not pay you for how much you know but for how useful your knowledge is in helping them achieve their goals."

Remember, people don't care how much you know (productive wealth) until they know how much you care (relational wealth.) Spending productive wealth in the right way is wisdom. Wisdom means to know how, when, in what way and why. It fully integrates knowledge, skills, talents, gifts, experience, and deep understanding of life's ups and downs.

5. Spiritual wealth
To build life wealth, we must invest our spiritual wealth. This the authority and power we receive from our relationship with God.

 Jesus demonstrated this power in his ministry. In fact, Jesus stated that he could no nothing unless it was to be shown by the Father. (John 5:19,20) He invested his relational wealth and his physical wealth in time with the Father to produce spiritual wealth. People listening to Jesus were "astonished at his teaching, for his word possessed authority." (Luke 4:32)

Jesus had an abundance of spiritual wealth, which enabled him to carry out His mission. Jesus constantly encouraged people to invest all they had to gain spiritual wealth.
"The kingdom of heaven is like treasure hidden in a field, which a man found and covered up. Then in his joy he goes and sells all that he has and buys that field." (Matthew 13:44) It is worth spending all you have, to gain spiritual wealth.

The goal of the disciple is to grow your spiritual wealth, to invest the other four wealths (financial, physical, productive, and relational) to build up spiritual wealth which is the most important. Well Done – Part 3: Multiplying Your Resources

Investing spiritual wealth is the essential way to grow the other four.
Think about another economic metaphor Jesus used. He said that a relationship with Him – and with the Father through Him – is like finding *"a pearl of great price,"* which far exceeded the value of anything else. It's like finding a treasure in a field and being smart enough to liquidate everything so you can buy the field. That's Jesus' message to us about the value of spiritual wealth: it's far more valuable than our money. We will do well to sell everything to get it. Cash it all in for that one thing that is most valuable. It just makes good economic sense! Would you be willing to follow God's leading if He presented you with such an opportunity? Where is your treasure? Is it in the security and comfort of your wealth on earth or in the loving arms of your heavenly Father who richly provides all you need? Spiritual wealth is concerned with how much spiritual wealth we have to invest. The currency is fruit that will last.

In order to build spiritual wealth, we need to invest wealth from our other four accounts. We might take time off work to travel to a conference or meet with someone who could help us grow our spiritual wealth. We can buy (investing financial wealth) and read books that will assist in developing our spiritual wealth. We can offer our skills and knowledge to an organization (investing productive wealth) that could help us grow our spiritual wealth. Perhaps we offer time to serve someone (investing physical wealth) who can help us grow our spiritual wealth. This is actually the very thing the disciples did with Jesus. The disciples were investing their financial, relational, productive, and physical wealth to enable Jesus to invest His spiritual wealth in them.

There are all kinds of other ways to invest to see spiritual wealth grown. We could choose to spend more time (investing physical wealth) in prayer and Bible study for a season. We can ask friends and family for their wisdom in situations and circumstances (investing relational wealth).

DAY 18: QUESTIONS TO PONDER

153

How have you seen God multiply resources either in your life or in the life of others?

Which of the five wealths resonated most with you and why?

What will happen if one of the five wealths is much larger than the others?

DAY 19: HOW MUCH IS ENOUGH?

KEY VERSE

"And God is able to make all grace overflow to you so that because you have enough of everything in every way at all times, you will overflow in every good work."

1 Corinthians 9:8

H ow much is enough? This question is very easy to ask but difficult to answer. The answer, however, leads us to realize the most important things in life. The Greek philosopher Epicurus stated, "Nothing is enough for the man to whom enough is too little." Contrast that with J.D. Rockefeller's well-known answer. Although stated over a hundred years ago, the richest man in the world at the time seems to have characterized our wealth system recently. "How much is enough? Just a little bit more!"

Joseph Heller, author of the excellent novel *Catch-22*, was at a party in New York thrown by a billionaire for a bunch of writers. Someone asked him how it made him feel that no matter how successful he was as an author, he would never make the kind of money his host did. Heller replied, "I have something he will never have. And that's the knowledge that I have enough."

Seth Godin writes, "If your happiness is based on always getting a littlo more than you've got...then you've handed control of your happiness to the gatekeepers ...You are always on the treadmill, unhappy today, imagining that the answer lies just over the next hill. All the data shows us that the people on that hill are just as frustrated as the people on your hill...The never-ending cycle (no surprise) never ends." [45]

The gatekeepers of our modern culture move us down the road of economic advancement, which economists and politicians have honestly believed to be the solution to humanity's problems. The conveniences I enjoy and the lifestyle I want to maintain make me a beneficiary of such

thinking. Yet if we are honest with ourselves, we should admit that the economic road was never suggested to us by Christ. Most of what people really want in life – love, friendship, respect, family, standing, fun – cannot be bought and do not pass through the market. The proverbial "bottom line" is not actually the bottom line we're after at the deepest level.

Instead of bringing true satisfaction, the longing for more brings us, according to Mother Teresa, deep dissatisfaction instead. She said, "Once the longing for money comes, the longing also comes for what money can give: superfluities, nice rooms, luxuries at table, more clothes, fans, and so on. Our needs will increase, for one thing brings another, and the result will be endless dissatisfaction." [46]

A. W. Tozer wrote that what comes into our minds when we think about God is the most important thing about us. People today want a God who will satisfy all our needs, keep us from suffering, make us happy, and enable us to buy everything we want. Our all-embracing preoccupation with consumerism has affected the way we think about God. Our image of God has become a kind of Amazon, able to provide all we need, when we need it, in 24 hours. Or less.

THE LAW OF DIMINISHING RETURNS

The law of diminishing returns says, "The tendency for a continuing application of effort or skill toward a particular project or goal declines in effectiveness after a certain level of result has been achieved."The law of diminishing returns can be illustrated by what I call the fulfillment curve. This curve takes us through four stages of spending and reflects the degree of fulfillment experienced at each stage.

STAGE 1

Law of Diminishing Returns

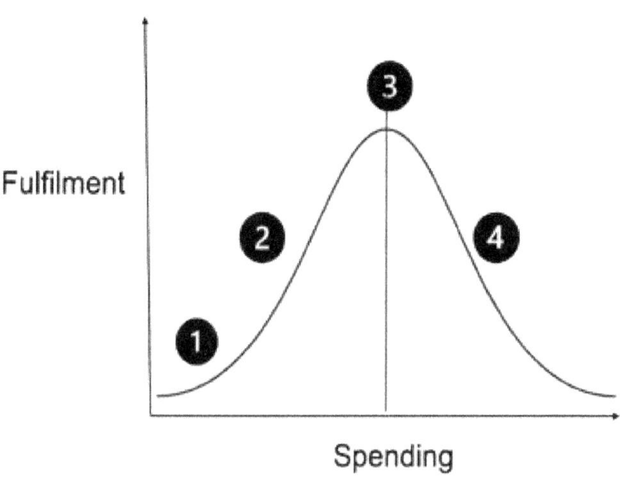

If we plot fulfillment against money spent, we see first a sharp rise in fulfillment with the ability to spend to meet basic needs. Of course, the Lord has promised to meet our basic needs and urged us not to be anxious about them. *"Therefore I tell you, do not be anxious about your life, what you will eat or what you will drink, nor about your body, what you will put on. Is not life more than food, and the body more than clothing?"* (Matthew 6:25).

He feeds the birds of the air, and clothes the lilies of the field. We are told to "seek first the kingdom of God and his righteousness, and all these things will be added to you" (Matthew 6:33). What are "all these things?" Based on the context of this promise, I believe them to be everything we need for daily living.

With these provided, we then need to learn to be content. "But if we have food and clothing, with these we will be content" (1 Timothy 6:8).

The secret to building wealth is to learn to be content with what we have. "Keep your life free from love of money, and be content with what you have, for he has said, 'I will never
leave you nor forsake you'" (Hebrews 13:5). Being content with our daily needs and thanking God for His provision forms a foundation on which He can build. We are then not focused on money or the lack of it but solely on His provision, whether we feel it is enough or not. He promises to give us sufficient for our needs and for all He asks us to do. Complaining about our current financial state is a lack of faith and disrespectful to the Lord. He never makes mistakes but will always provide for everything He asks us to do.

Contentment is a secret to be learned. "I know how to be brought low, and I know how to abound. In any and every circumstance, I have learned the secret of facing plenty and hunger, abundance and need. I can do all things through him who strengthens me" (Philippians 4:12-13).

STAGE 2

The curve continues to rise as we spend on basic comforts if and when we can afford it. This is quite a normal and good way to spend. The Lord wants us to enjoy a comfortable life, enjoying what He and people have created. "As for the rich in this present age, charge them not to be haughty, nor to set
their hopes on the uncertainty of riches, but on God, who richly provides us with everything to enjoy" (1 Timothy 6:17).

We can be thankful for a nice home, a good car, a wonderful vacation, and many other nice things of life. For me, the key is to plan this spending in prayer. *"Delight yourself in the LORD, and he will give you the desires of your heart"* (Psalm 37:4).
I understand this to mean that if I look to the Lord, recognizing His ownership of everything I have in my possession and His authority over my life, I can ask Him for many good things and He will lay on my heart what I can trust Him for. I
t's not that He will provide everything my heart desires, but rather He will put on my heart what to desire from Him; what I should be

desiring and asking Him for. "And this is the confidence that we have toward him, that if we ask anything according to his will he hears us. And if we know that he hears us in whatever we ask, we know that we have the requests that we have asked of him" (1 John 5:14-15).

STAGE 3

This stage, at the top of the curve, signifies maximum fulfillment. It is the answer to the question, How much is enough? After this point, extra spending does not yield more satisfaction. We have reached the apex, the point at which our lifestyle has become a reflection of the prayer of Agur; ". . . give me neither poverty nor riches; feed me with the food that is needful for me, lest I be full and deny you and say, 'Who is the LORD?' or lest I be poor and steal and profane the name of my God" (Proverbs 30:8-9).

This is a prayer for contentment and fulfillment of life in either poverty or riches. The problem with riches is that we can become complacent, self-sufficient, not thinking we need God because we have so much. The problem with poverty is that we can start cutting corners, trying to get money unlawfully, disrespecting God, and denying His ability to provide. The prayer is essentially, "Lord, give me what is needful for me: That's how much 'enough' is!"

This is a key stage of spending, when we reach maximum fulfillment. Recognizing when we are there comes as a result of the prayer, "Lord feed me with the food that is needful for me."

STAGE 4

Stage 4 transitions into spending more on luxuries. The fulfillment return on our extra spending tails off as we move into consumerism and overconsumption.

Looking at what King Solomon spent on himself and the conclusions he made about his life, we can see that spending on luxuries does not bring deep satisfaction. "I said in my heart,

'Come now, I will test you with pleasure; enjoy yourself.' But behold, this also was vanity" (Ecclesiastes 2:1). He concluded, "And whatever my eyes desired I did not keep from them. I kept my heart from no pleasure, for my heart found pleasure in all my toil, and this was my reward for all my toil. Then I considered all that my hands had done and the toil I had expended in doing it, and behold, all was vanity and a striving after wind, and there was nothing to be gained under the sun" (Ecclesiastes 2:10-11).

When we reach the top of the fulfillment curve at Stage 3, we have arrived at a good finish line for our spending. How then, can we use the surplus money to increase our fulfillment as believers? The answer is to invest more in God's kingdom. Jesus said, *". . . It is more blessed to give than to receive"* (Acts 20:35). In other words, when you are at the stage that you can invest more in God's work among people, you will be more fulfilled. The Greek work for "blessed" is *"makarios,"* which carries the meaning of complete, whole, all together. It is the Greek equivalent of the Hebrew "shalom."

Henry David Thoreau stated, "It is preoccupation with possessions, more than anything else, that prevents us from living freely and nobly." Limiting our consumption and determining how much is enough can then give us the ability to spend money on building wealth to invest in doing good.

SIMPLE LIVING

Contemporary culture is plagued by the passion to possess. These days, all seem to believe that the good life is found in accumulation, that more is better. The complexity of rushing to achieve and accumulate more and more frequently threatens to overwhelm us; it seems there is no escape from the rat race. And remember that in the rat race, only rats win!

In the midst of the Nazi terror, Dietrich Bonhoeffer said, "To be simple is to fix one's eye solely on the simple truth of God at a time when all concepts are being confused, distorted, and turned upside-down."

The focus on simple living frees us from this modern mania. It brings sanity to our compulsive extravagance, and peace to our frantic spirit.

The Christian discipline of simplicity is an inward reality that results in an outward lifestyle. Simplicity sets us free to receive the provision of God as a gift that is not ours to keep and can be freely shared with others.

The focus of the discipline of simplicity is to "seek first the kingdom of God and his righteousness, and all these things will be added to you" (Matthew 6:33). If we seek the interests of the kingdom above all else, the Lord will provide all we need to live as His children and to accomplish the tasks He sets us to do.

How can we develop "simple living"? In his great book *Freedom of Simplicity*, Richard Foster proposes ten steps to develop an outward expression of the inward discipline of simplicity. [47]

1. Buy things for their usefulness rather than their status.
2. Reject anything that is producing an addiction in you.
3. Develop a habit of giving things away.
4. Refuse to be propagandized by the custodians of modern gadgetry.
5. Learn to enjoy things without owning them.
6. Develop a deeper appreciation for the creation.
7. Look with a healthy skepticism at all "buy now, pay later" schemes.
8. Obey Jesus' instructions about plain, honest speech (Matthew 5:37).
9. Reject anything that breeds the oppression of others.
10. Shun anything that distracts you from seeking first the kingdom of God.

I would like to humbly add an eleventh: Learn to be content.

CONTENTMENT

Being content with what we have goes hand in hand with simple living.
To develop the art of contentment, we need to ask God to change our hearts and the way we think. We need to ask Him to keep us focused on His ways instead of the world's ways. "Don't copy the behavior and customs of this world, but let God transform you into a new person by changing the way you think. Then you will learn to know God's will for you, which is good and pleasing and perfect" (Romans 12:2, NLT).

Contentment is a secret to be learned. ". . . I have learned to be content whatever the circumstances. I know what it is to be in need, and I know what it is to have plenty. I have learned the secret of being content in any and every situation, whether well fed or hungry, whether living in plenty or in want. I can do all this through him who gives me strength" (Philippians 4:11-13, NIV).
So, how can we practically learn this secret and learn contentment? Paul provides us with some insight in 1 Thessalonians 5:16-18 (NIV). *"Rejoice always, pray continually, give thanks in all circumstances; for this is God's will for you in Christ Jesus."*
We should choose joy, knowing that the Lord is in control of any and every situation.
We should pray continually, focusing our minds on God and His provision. Whatever we focus our minds on will have a profound impact on our actions and attitude.
We should give thanks in all circumstances, no matter what, as an acknowledgement of God's lordship over our lives. God has blessed us more than we realize. What we appreciate
– appreciates!

Developing contentment is building wealth! *"Godliness with contentment is great gain"* (1 Timothy 6:6). We build spiritual wealth because contentment allows us to remain focused on God and ignore worldly materialism. We can build material wealth, because as we learn to decrease our spending on consumer items, we save more to achieve our long-term goals and to be generous.

Contentment is not the fulfillment of our wants but appreciation of what God has given us and the freedom to share this with others. I find this a huge challenge. My practice is to make a spending plan that sets a limit on spending, and then I regularly evaluate my obligations and needs. We will discuss this in our next Day's reading.

Before that, I would like to introduce you to someone who set limits on his spending and was able to build great wealth.

DR. TOBY ORD

"The £33,000 a year Oxford Don giving £1 million to African Aid!" [48] I was astonished to read this headline in English newspapers in November of 2009. What a life goal! I asked myself, How is this possible? As an academic earning £33,000 a year, Toby Ord is in an unlikely position to give £1million to charity. But the Oxford University researcher at 30 years of age has pledged to donate a large portion of his lifetime earnings to save lives in Africa.

The report went on to say that he will sacrifice a big house, fast cars, and foreign travel to give a large proportion of his salary to small charities that buy and administer drugs to treat those suffering from TB and tropical diseases. He is starting by living on £20,000 of his annual salary and giving the rest away. Dr. Ord calculates that, allowing for inflation and pay raises, he will be able to hit his £1million target. He estimates his salary from Oxford's Balliol College will average £42,000 over the remaining 35 years of his career. The amount of salary he keeps will also rise in line with inflation.

He said: "Many people agree that global poverty is one of the biggest moral problems of our time, but very few people are prepared to donate a large part of their income to help eliminate it. I decided to put my money where my mouth is and to set up an association for people who want to join me. Ideally it will become a well-recognized way of living one's life . . ."

Dr. Ord lives in a one-bedroom rented flat on the grounds of Balliol College in Oxford. He said, "I did all the calculations and realized I could save the lives of thousands. Saving just one person's life is often thought to be an amazing kind of thing you can do over your whole career."

Dr. Ord has launched a group called Giving What We Can to encourage others to donate at least ten percent of their pre-tax income to the development aid charities of their choice. So far 23 people have signed up for this lifetime commitment.
The pledge states: "I recognize that I can use part of my income to do a significant amount of good in the developing world. Since I can live well enough on a smaller income, I pledge that from today until the day I retire, I shall give at least ten percent of what I earn to whichever organizations can most effectively use it to fight poverty in the developing world. I make this pledge freely, openly and without regret."

Donations from the Giving What We Can community totaled more than £7 million at the end of 2014. In April 2021, the community has over 5,000 members who have pledged to donate over $2.5 billion over the course of their careers. They have already given more than $220 million! [49]
Dr. Toby Ord answered the question of how much is enough for himself and stopped spending at stage 3 of our fulfillment curve, giving away the rest with astounding consequences.
In the next Day, we will look at a practical way to answer the question of how much is enough for ourselves.

DAY 19: QUESTIONS TO PONDER

If someone asked you "How much is enough?" how would you respond?

What would be your top three steps to develop simple living from Richard Foster's list?

How are you developing the art of contentment?

DAY 20: YOUR FINANCIAL CIRCLE

KEY VERSE

"Therefore do not be anxious, saying, 'What shall we eat?' or 'What shall we drink?' or 'What shall we
wear?' For the Gentiles seek after all these things, and your heavenly Father knows that you need them all."

Matthew 6:31-32

Money is the language of the world, and God's word is the translation that leads to true financial freedom. "Money makes the world go round," and God's word makes me able to navigate the troubled seas.

Managing money is not just a matter of adding, subtracting, or working with percentages; that's easy! Managing money is more of a spiritual discipline because it has to do with our character, priorities, and values. I must confess I am a spender rather than a saver. I like buying things. Fortunately, I have a wife who is very frugal and always looking for bargains. I have learned that spending without a plan is a recipe for disaster. I have experienced firsthand what the wise Solomon so graphically describes. *"In the blink of an eye wealth disappears, for it will sprout wings and fly away like an eagle"* (Proverbs 23:5, NLT).

This seems to have been a problem in Old Testament times. The prophet Haggai relayed God's words: *"Now, therefore, thus says the Lord of hosts: Consider your ways. You have sown much and harvested little. You eat, but you never have enough; you drink, but you never have your fill. You clothe yourselves, but no one is warm. And he who earns wages does so to put them into a bag with holes"* (Haggai 1:5-6). Haggai is speaking to people who spent sixteen years building personal prosperity with the end result being loss

and failure. God is asking us today to reconsider our ways; He wants us to focus on building His house.
He is inviting us to adjust our lives to His way of managing our money. Haggai's picture of bags with holes is a powerful image that reflects our experience. Where does the money go? I always seem to have more month than money!
God does not want us to just patch up our bags and wait for things to get back to normal. Instead, we must find a new way of living as faithful stewards of all He has given to us. Don't patch the bags; get new bags!

In our reading today, we will look at making a new bag by using the concept of a "financial circle of enough." The only way to make a line's ends meet is to form a circle. It's always great to be able to make ends meet, but it's even nicer if you can make them meet in a bow. Forming your financial circle is a way of developing a spending plan or budget and limiting your spending so that you have some left over for the nice bow! We are using the words "spending plan" and "budget" interchangeably because they both mean the same thing, but a spending plan sounds much nicer!

The word "budget" is derived from the French "*bougette*," a diminutive form of "*bouge*," a leather bag. Its first meaning in English was pouch, wallet, or bag, containing money. Its first meaning in English was pouch, wallet, or bag. Many people associate the word "budget" with restriction, hard work, and discipline. However, making a budget and sticking to it provides great rewards. It is an essential tool for planning your financial life together with God.
The secret to building financial wealth is very easy. Spend less than you earn over a long period of time, and you will be financially successful. To do this, set up a spending plan, together with God – the owner of your money – to ensure that each month you are spending less than is coming in.

Then you'll have the opportunity to build discipline in sticking to your plan and saying no to unbudgeted items. Referring back to the fruit of the Spirit in Part 2 of this book, we see that the only way to pull this off long-term is through the indwelling power of the Spirit, who empowers us with self-control, patience, etc.

How do I make ends meet when the ends seem to be getting longer? The concept of a closed circle has helped me free up extra money in order to be generous.

YOUR FINANCIAL CIRCLE

 Your financial circle is simply a way of portioning your income into three main categories: your obligations, your needs, and your wants. Obligations are fixed costs that are generally the same each month and easy to plan. These encompass such spending as giving, mortgage or rent, water and energy, transportation, insurances, communication, and online subscriptions. Needs are variable expenses such as food, clothing, personal care, and entertainment. Your wants are larger purchases for which you need to save, like furniture, house maintenance, car purchase, vacations, etc.

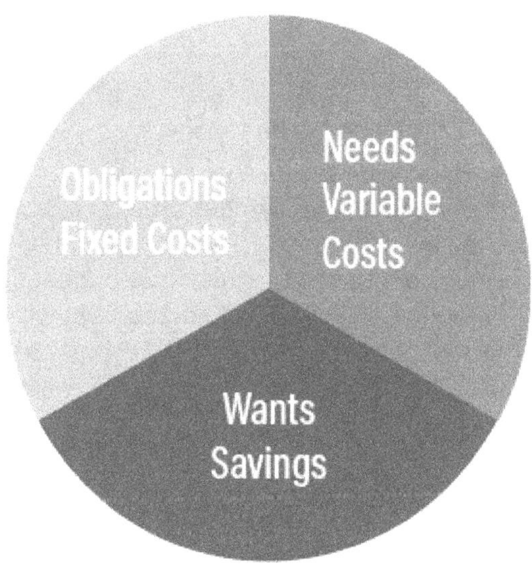

The details of your circle will be unique, just as your circumstances, responsibilities, and plans are not exactly like anyone else's. The size of each slice may vary considerably; this simple graph is not meant to imply that they should be equal in size. The point is simply to illustrate the idea of a circle containing the main categories of your spending.

A CIRCLE OF PROMISE

The circle has many benefits that are worth highlighting. First, it is a circle of promise. Jesus promises that if you "Seek first the kingdom of God and his righteousness, all these things will be added to you" (Matthew 6:33). So, what are *"all these things"*? They are everything you need to enjoy the life God has given you and to do all He asks you to do! They are everything you need to fulfill the roles He has called you to perform in life. We all seem to be pretty good at spending time and money on things we need, but we often ignore or overlook activities God wants us to do.

A CIRCLE OF PEACE

The circle is also a circle of peace. When we live in the circle of peace, we are free from worry and anxiety, free from fear of an uncertain future. Biblical peace is *"shalom,"* which means wholeness, completeness. Living in the circle of peace, or shalom, means that we can live a balanced life in which our spending reflects the priorities of our hearts. This circle of peace keeps us free from loving money, enabling us to be content with whatever we have. *"Keep your life free from love of money, and be content with what you have, for he has said, 'I will never leave you nor forsake you'"* (Hebrews 13:5).

A CIRCLE OF PROVISION

The circle of provision enjoys and is thankful for all God provides. Our Lord God is called *"Jehovah Jireh"* or *"the God who provides."*

Paul could confidently tell the Christians in Philippi, "My God will supply every need of yours according to his riches in glory in Christ Jesus" (Philippians 4:19).

A CIRCLE OF PROTECTION

When we live in the circle of protection, we can be assured of God's protection. "I have been young, and now am old, yet I have not seen the righteous forsaken or his children begging for bread" (Psalm 37:25). God promises that if we honor Him by giving the tithe, the first tenth of our income, He will protect the rest. "I will rebuke the devourer for you, so that it will not destroy the fruits of your soil, and your vine in the field shall not fail to bear, says the Lord of hosts" (Malachi 3:11).

A CIRCLE OF PLENTY

Lastly, we are developing a circle of plenty, of abundance. God does not merely want to provide whatever we need; He desires to give us more than enough so we can bless others. *"And God is able to make all grace abound to you, so that having all sufficiency in all things at all times, you may abound in every good work"* (2 Corinthians 9:8).

A CLOSED CIRCLE

The concept of closing your circle means to limit your expenditures by making a plan – in prayer together with God and your partner if you have one. Closing your circle says, "Lord, if you will provide what we have agreed, then that is enough for me to do all you are asking me to do. I thank you for what you are providing, and I will be content with it. If you give me more, I will not spend it all on myself but will use the excess for good works, to bless my family and extend your kingdom."

On the basis of God owning it all, I have to ask tough questions. My prayer ought to be, "Lord, what do you want me to do with **your** money? How much of **your** money should I spend on myself?"

DESIGNING YOUR OWN CIRCLE – A PARTNERSHIP WITH GOD

 In managing our finances, God has a part to play, and I have a part to play. Both have unique rights and responsibilities. I can never do what only God can do, and He will not do what I must do.
God's part is to give us assignments, using money to carry out His wishes. *"Calling ten of his servants, he gave them ten minas, and said to them, 'Engage in business until I come'"* (Luke 19:13). God always pays for what He orders!

A second part of God's unique role is providing for our needs and the needs of those around us. The same Lord who provided manna in the desert cared also for Elijah in his time of need. "You shall drink from the brook, and I have commanded the ravens to feed you there. And the ravens brought him bread and meat in the morning, and bread and meat in the evening, and he drank from the brook" (1 Kings 17:4,6).
A third aspect of God's role in finances is to use money to test us: can He trust us with greater responsibilities? "If you are faithful in little things, you will be faithful in large ones. But if you are dishonest in little things, you won't be honest with greater responsibilities" (Luke 16:10, NLT).

My part is using what He has entrusted to me faithfully, according to His wishes. *"And if you are untrustworthy about worldly wealth, who will trust you with the true riches of heaven?"* (Luke 16:11, NLT). To carry out His wishes, we must find out what they are through prayer and following the instructions given to us in the Bible.

AN OPEN CIRCLE

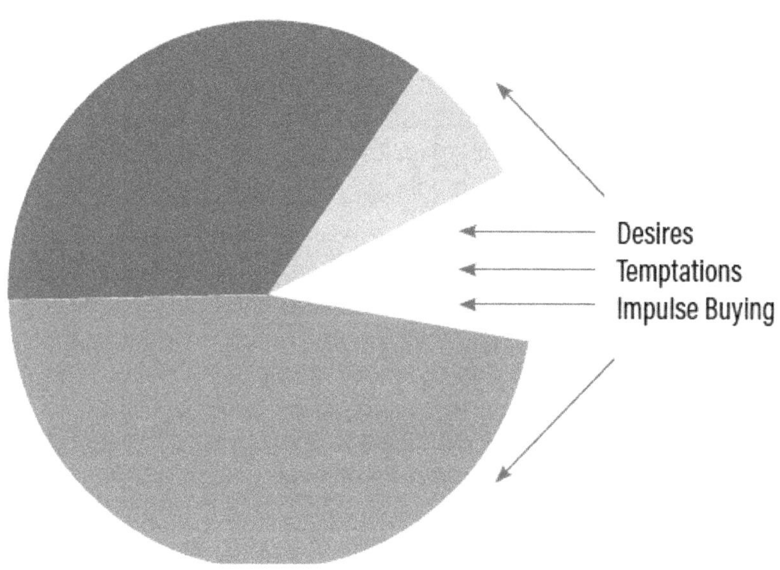

 Once I have made my spending plan according to my priorities and apportioned my income into the various categories, closing the circle means to stop additional spending. Set a finish line. We will constantly be tempted to expand our lifestyle to consume all available income!

Since repetition is one of our most effective learning strategies, I am repeating the next few key sentences from Part 2. Outside inducements such as advertising and peer pressure as well as the inside temptations of greed and emotional insecurity will lead us to spend more on our lifestyle – which is ever expanding and needs ever-increasing financing! We need to say no to these voices of the world's system that constantly tempt us to increase our spending. If I give into the world's standards, I will not be able to fulfill God's purpose for my life – to be generous and reach my life goals.

"Do not love the world or the things in the world. If anyone loves the world, the love of the Father is not in him. For all that is in the world – the desires of the flesh and the desires of the eyes and pride of life – is not from the Father but is from the world. And the world is passing away along with its desires, but whoever does the will of God abides forever" (1 John 2:15-17).

Living in an open circle means that you have not put a limit on your expenses. When you focus on desires and buying more and more, the circle expands. Everything that comes in, goes out – and then some. When spending exceeds income, nasty things happen. You may have to borrow and go into debt, thereby limiting your freedom. You may say, "I can't afford to give any more. I need the money." Pressure on the budget could even lead to dishonesty and cheating on expenses or taxes. When soldiers came to John the Baptist and asked, *"What shall we do?"* John answered, *"Do not extort money from anyone by threats or by false accusation, and be content with your wages"* (Luke 3:14).

If we are living in, by, and through the Spirit, we will overcome any and all of these pressures because we are playing a completely different game. The goal is not the accumulation of stuff. Instead, *"I press on toward the goal for the prize of the upward call of God in Christ Jesus"* (Philippians 3:14). I do my spending then in the light of eternity.

THE 20 PERCENT TEST

I would suggest using a 20 percent test to determine whether your lifestyle is appropriate and God honoring. Take your overall monthly spending level and ask yourself the two following questions.

First, if you increased spending by 20 percent, what would you add to your lifestyle? Are these new additions worthwhile, enhancing your ability to live out your calling and to honor God? Are they worth allocating funds to, when the same funds could be saved or given now to build Christ's kingdom?

Second, if you cut spending by 20 percent, what would you eliminate? Is keeping these things worthwhile by the standard stated above?

This exercise may require careful consideration. Take time to sit down and write out the implications; we believe that careful evaluation of one's budget is a required act of sound stewardship. The importance of closing your circle, to make sure that at the very least you are not living outside of your harvest, was stated famously by Wilkins Micawber in Charles Dickens's *David Copperfield*. "Annual income twenty pounds, annual expenditure nineteen, nineteen and six, result happiness.

Annual income twenty pounds, annual expenditure twenty pounds naught and six, result misery."

AN OVERFLOWING CIRCLE

Once the circle has been closed and you have said to the Lord, "This is enough for me and my family," you may have more coming in than you really need for daily living; many do. If you set a finish line for your spending, the rest can overflow. Overflow can be achieved in two ways. First, by earning more. Second, by reducing spending. Earning more is generally much more difficult to achieve than spending less. If your circle is closed, then any income you do not need for the three areas flows over.

When planning your finances with God, you can trust His ability to provide more than you need. "And God is able to make all grace abound to you, so that having all sufficiency in all things at all times, you may abound in every good work" (2 Corinthians 9:8). His grace will provide sufficient to live on

and then enough to *"abound in every good work."* Overflow is purposed for these good works. God also stated that giving would lead to abundance. *"Give, and it will be given to you.*
Good measure, pressed down, shaken together, running over, will be put into your lap. For with the measure you use it will be measured back to you" (Luke 6:38).

The Lord will not release this abundance to be spent on an ever-increasing lifestyle. He does not put money into a "bag with holes." It will be released when we limit spending on ourselves and use the abundance to bless others. When my circle is closed, I can start asking the Lord for overflow.
A condition for overflow is being faithful to use His money in His

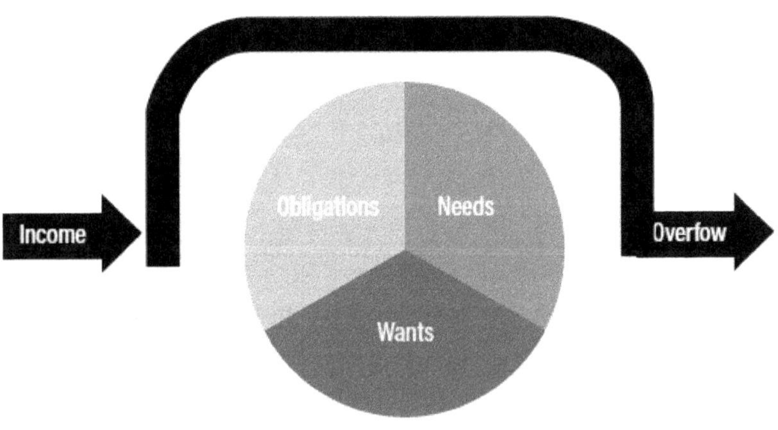

way for His purposes. Jesus said, "If then you have not been faithful in the unrighteous wealth, who will entrust to you the true riches?" (Luke 16:11).
Jesus stated very clearly that the measure by which He can trust us with what He called, "true riches" is determined

by how faithful we are in using the money He has already entrusted to us. True riches encompass *"treasures in heaven,"* an intimate relationship with Christ, and seeing others come to Christ.

NET SPENDABLE INCOME

Our circle reflects how we manage our net spendable income, which is our income after taxes and tithe.
Jesus gave a brilliant answer to some religious leaders who tried to trap him with a question about paying taxes to the Roman occupation government.
"Is it lawful to pay taxes to Caesar, or not? Should we pay it, or not?" Jesus knew that they were hypocrites trying to trick Him. He answered, "Show me a denarius. Whose likeness and inscription does it have?" They said, 'Caesar's.' He said to them, 'Then render to Caesar the things that are Caesar's, and to God the things that are God's'" (Luke 20:24-25).
They were amazed at His answer.

What belongs to God? Everything! If you realize that everything in this world – including all of Caesar's rights, power, and possessions – belongs to God, then you can give, without difficulty, *"to Caesar what is Caesar's."*

If you know that everything belongs to God, then whatever you give to the emperor, you will give in the name of God. Any authority you grant to the emperor, you grant to him for the sake of God's greater authority. Any authority you grant to the emperor, you grant to him out of the greater authority of God. You obey Caesar, when this stems from the need to obey what God wants us to do. What is Caesar's is determined by God's permission.

What is Caesar's is determined by the fact that everything is God's and becomes Caesar's only by God's permission and intention. This is why Peter says, *"Be subject for the Lord's sake to every human institution, whether it be to the emperor as supreme, or to governors as sent by him . . ."* (1 Peter 2:13-14).

Paul wrote very clearly to the believers in Rome, "Let every person be subject to the governing authorities. For there is no authority except from God, and those that exist have been instituted by God. Therefore, whoever resists the authorities resists what God has appointed, and those who resist will incur judgment" (Romans 13:1-2).
He concludes, "For because of this you also pay taxes, for the authorities are ministers of God, attending to this very thing" (Romans 13:6). We must be honest and diligent in our tax returns. It is a spiritual discipline for the reasons mentioned above.
Since everything belongs to God, including the money we receive for our labor, the first part of our harvest also belongs to God. When we honor the Lord's ownership, we give Him the firstfruits of our harvest, which represent the tithe, or ten percent of our income before the government takes its share. In my country, the government recognizes this and does not levy tax on the ten percent given to charitable causes.

When we give the firstfruits, the tithe, to the Lord, God promises to provide all we need. A believer should never say, "I can't afford to give the tithe." That is a statement of faithlessness.
Giving the tithe will also protect the rest of the money from being "devoured." "Bring the full tithe into the storehouse, that there may be food in my house. And thereby put me to the test, says the Lord of hosts . . . I will rebuke the devourer for you so that it will not destroy the fruits of your soil . . ." (Malachi 3:10-11). I believe the "devourer" to be our adversary, the devil, who wants us to get tied up in consumerism that never brings true satisfaction.

DAY 20: QUESTIONS TO PONDER

If you increased spending by 20 percent, what would you add to your lifestyle?

Are these new additions worthwhile, enhancing your ability to live out your calling to honor God?

If you cut spending by 20 percent, what would you eliminate?

How would keeping these things enhance or detract from living out your calling to honor God?

DAY 21: FAITH FINANCIAL PLANNING

KEY VERSE

"The plans of the heart belong to man, but the answer of the tongue is from the Lord. All the ways of a man are pure in his own eyes, but the Lord weighs the spirit. Commit your work to the Lord, and your plans will be established."

Proverbs 16:1-3

What is faith financial planning? Planning our finances is a partnership with God, and we are told that *"whatever does not proceed from faith is sin"* (Romans 14:23). So, what is faith? Again, the Bible tells us, "Now faith is the assurance of things hoped for, the conviction of things not seen" (Hebrews 11:1).

Faith financial planning has everything to do with an eternal perspective, planning our finances to have the most eternal impact. "And without faith it is impossible to please him, for whoever would draw near to God must believe that he exists and that he rewards those who seek him" (Hebrews 11:6). Financial faith planning is drawing near to God and planning for the eternal reward.

SET GOALS

When the Lord gives us more than enough, when our circle is overflowing, it is important to set goals for how we will use the surplus financial assets.

Goal setting is extremely important. Finances always involve a tradeoff between the short-term and the long-term. If we don't have long-term goals, we simply won't know how to prioritize our spending and saving in the short-term. Money is a tool. to

accomplish other goals and objectives, and setting goals gives us clarity about how to use this tool – money – toward our savings, debt repayment, budgeting, or giving.
Having written goals makes it far more likely that we will be disciplined and maintain good financial habits. Habits take root in our lives when we have a strong "why" motivating them.
Goals provide the why, the necessary motivation. In some ways, written goals close the loop with all the other beneficial financial habits we develop.

Knowing why we are doing something via a written goal helps us create a starting point, stay the course, and know when we are done and can look to new goals. Proverbs 29:18 says, *"Where there is no vision, the people are unrestrained"* (NASB). Writing goals is a way to clarify the vision God has given us for our lives. Pursuing them provides a pathway and helps us make more confident decisions today.

As followers of Christ, we are privileged to be able to set goals with God's input and vision. One of my favorite verses says "For we are His creation, created in Christ Jesus for good works, which God prepared ahead of time so that we should walk in them" (Ephesians 2:10, HCSB). God has already prepared works for us to do. When we ask Him to speak into our goals, He can move us into those works and allow us the privilege of completing them. Without goals, our financial decisions are dictated by other people, unchecked emotions, and perceived urgency – all of which obstruct wise decision making. Most of us operate by simply accumulating as much as we can, which is the world's way of thinking. Since the longing for more is insatiable, we never experience financial peace and rest.

Only a Christian has the ability to set faith goals and ask, "God what do you want me to achieve?" This is a way to experience the hand of God in my financial situation. A faith goal is a statement: "I believe that God is calling me to___"
(fill in the blank). I need to be wholeheartedly committed to internalizing and acting on this statement.

I believe goals (1) give direction and purpose, (2) help crystallize thinking, and (3) provide personal motivation.
In building confidence that God will direct my steps, it helps to visualize the sequence.

1. My goal setting comes from God.

2. I seek His will and His wisdom.

3. I start to move.

4. He directs my steps.

"The plans of the heart belong to man, but the answer of the tongue is from the Lord. All the ways of a man are pure in his own eyes, but the Lord weighs the spirit. Commit your work to the Lord, and your plans will be established" (Proverbs 16:1-3).

Setting long-term goals while you are young is vitally important. If you don't, years go by without appropriate intermediate steps, and you eventually end up dealing with long-term goals as though they were short-term because short-term is all you have left. Long-term goals are much more difficult to finance on a short-term basis, but setting aside a small amount over a long period will help you build assets to meet them.
Planning my finances with God, together with my wife, has been a rewarding exercise to help realize my long-term goals.

THE PROCESS OF FAITH FINANCIAL PLANNING

The process of financial planning is simplified in the following five-stage illustration.

Our first responsibility is to recognize that the Lord will provide all we need for all He asks us to do. When Abraham was tested to see if he would obey God by sacrificing his most precious son, the Lord rewarded his willingness by providing a ram to be sacrificed. Abraham attributed to God the name Jehovah Jireh, which means *"The Lord will provide."*
 We read in Genesis 22:14, "So Abraham called the name of that place, "The LORD will provide"; as it is said to this day, "On the mount of the LORD it shall be provided."
His provision is the harvest we can gather, our gross income.

"And God is able to make all grace abound to you, so that having all sufficiency in all things at all times, you may abound in every good work. As it is written, "He has distributed freely, he has given to the poor; his righteousness endures forever. He who supplies seed to the sower and bread for food will supply and multiply your seed for sowing and increase the harvest of your righteousness" (2 Corinthians 9:8-10).
The harvest consists not only of bread for food, which represents all we need for daily living but also seed to sow, representing money to invest, both in good works and
in generosity.

Step 1 in financial faith planning is to plan our taxes and tithes.
 The goals in Step 1 are to put aside God's part first and return the tithe to whom it belongs. It includes the commitment to be honest and diligent in our tax returns.
If you are a salaried employee, your taxes are deducted by your employer. However, the government allows some deductions for special expenses like health or charitable
giving. Businesses and self-employed people may claim tax benefits for certain business expenses.
It is essential that businesses and self-employed people plan for their taxes when these are not deducted each month. Business owners should be careful not to use money that should be reserved for taxes for operating or wealth expenditures.
Review the discussion about tithing in Day 20. Planning the tithe each month is one of our first disciplines of financial faith planning.

Step 2 is to plan what we need for daily living and short-term future needs. This is our circle of enough.

Faith financial planning means to define our circle, which is comprised broadly of three parts: (1) Our obligations, which are fixed expenses such as debt-repayments, rent or mortgage, insurances and other expenses that are roughly the same each month; (2) Variable expenses, which comprise money we spend on daily necessities; (3) Money we need to set aside for emergencies or saving for vacations, car purchase, or home necessities.

The goal in Step 2 is to answer the question, How much is enough? We'll give more detail on the circle of enough in the next Day.

Step 3 is planning to increase the overflow or margin, the difference between our net income (after tax and tithe) and the spending in our circle. We increase the overflow by increasing income, and/or by reducing spending to make the whole of the circle smaller. This overflow can then be used for longer- term goals (good works) and generosity.

"Precious treasure and oil are in a wise man's dwelling, but a foolish man devours it" (Proverbs 21:20).

The goal in Step 3 is to increase our margin and contain or reduce expenses, enabling us to both save and give, which will yield a great harvest later.

Step 4 is to invest in God's kingdom: to be generous with offers to advance His work among the poor and to make disciples in all nations. This will be discussed in "Multiplying resources" in our next Day's discussion. Our investment in Gods kingdom will be multiplied as He uses it to fulfill His purposes on earth.

The goal in Step 4 is to prime the pump, investing in kingdom projects and people, and experiencing multiplication of resources to advance the kingdom.

Step 5 is to use the remainder for our long-term goals. There are six broad categories of long-term goals.

1. Lifestyle desires such as a special vacation, second home, things of beauty, collections, or home

improvements. Remember, the Lord wants us to enjoy good things, as defined in prayer with Him.

2. Family needs like buying a home or helping your children or grandchildren buy a home, special needs for handicapped children, or being able to help parents in times of need.
3. Financial independence, which would enable you to retire from paid work to volunteer for charitable causes. This means that your resources will eventually generate enough income to fund all your short-term objectives excluding savings. If "enough" has been saved, you will no longer need short-term savings.
4. Freedom from debt, paying off long-term debt such as business borrowings or mortgages.
5. Saving for special charitable giving such as major donations or setting up a trust fund.
6. A new business with saved wealth or helping others start a business with risk wealth or loans.

The goal in Step 5 is to use the assets we have saved and invested to do good works, benefit our family, enjoy good things, and serve others.

It is so important to set goals for these long-term plans. Without setting a goal, a finish line, we keep accumulating. I talked to an accountant who told me that he is advising quite a few wealthy individuals who have enough to meet their long-term goals many times over. When we have reached our predetermined finish line by building assets sufficient to meet these goals, the surplus can be directed to extra generosity. More about financial finish lines in Day 23.

INCREASING MARGIN

 Restoring financial freedom requires putting first things first. The first thing – always – is to put God first. "But seek first the kingdom of God" [His priorities] "and His righteousness," [His way of doing things] *"and all these things will be added to you"* [you will experience His provision of all you need] (Matthew 6:33).

Richard Swenson, M.D., in his great book *Margin,* proposes a helpful list of steps for increasing our margin to build wealth.[50]

1.   COUNTER CULTURE.

To increase margin, we have to break radically with our culture which is shouting at us what we need in order to be accepted and successful. We are all caught up in a consumer culture; the most important economic indicator is 'spending power.' Dr. Swenson says, "It is rare to meet a person who isn't owned, bound, or trapped in destructive ways by a multitude of controlling cultural forces."
As I've been contemplating what most Christian financial ministries are teaching, it seems to me that most seem to focus on helping people 'achieve financial wealth' (live on a budget, have no debt, save up for retirement, etc). Is that the ultimate objective of what Jesus came to do? I don't think so. He came to save people from worldly and spiritual bondage, to help people think Biblically, act differently and then multiply this in the lives of others.

2.   LIVE WITHIN YOUR HARVEST.

To increase margin, we need the conviction that we should step out of the consumer merry-go-round and make do with what we have and be thankful for it! Going on a spending diet for a period of time will increase your financial health.
Living within your harvest seems to be restrictive, but it is exactly the opposite. Showing discipline in spending less than we earn, building up savings and investing for the future sets you free. Contentment and simplicity are invaluable friends in this effort, as we will see in the next two Days. We must learn to be content yourself with what God sends your way and live a simple life. If we are to increase our margin, we must put first things first. The first thing is, of course, to 'seek the Kingdom of God (His priorities) and His righteousness, (His way of doing things)' and then experience that 'all you need will be given to you.' (Matthew 6:33) When we out God's interests first, He will look after our harvest.

3.   DISCIPLINE DESIRES AND REDEFINE NEEDS.

Dr. Swenson noted that there is great confusion as to
Day 21: Faith Financial Planning how we distinguish needs from
desires. The list of what we call "needs" today is certainly much
longer than the list was in the time of our parents and
grandparents, let alone than in Jesus' days. If the list expands each
year, is this an expansion God approves of? We need to move from
consumerism to defining 'enough.'

4.   DECREASE SPENDING.

There are basically only three ways to increase our financial
margin; decrease spending, increase income, or increase savings.
By far the easiest is reducing spending. It sounds easy, but as we
all know, it's hard to sustain in practice. Our culture screams
against reducing spending, and every message we receive—from
the ads on television to the specials in the newspaper to our
neighbor's new van—all urge us to cave in.
Wear out whatever clothes you have in the closet. Make do with
whatever you have in the house. Remember the sampler on
Grandma's kitchen wall: "Use it up.Wear it out. Make it do. Do
without."

5.   INCREASE INCOME.

Increasing margin by increasing work hours is commonly used to
solve financial problems, however this can cause problems in
other areas of life. Relationships suffer, our physical health can be
seriously at risk, we could become less productive at our work
due to fatigue and our spiritual life may suffer die to lack of energy
and time. It may be much wiser to focus on reducing spending
and a simpler lifestyle than working longer hours. However, I have
known people to work two or three jobs for a concentrated period
of time to get out of serious debt situation quickly. Working in this
way should only be done for a specific purpose and a limited time.

6.   INCREASE SAVINGS.

Increasing savings is another way of maintaining financial margin. If you currently have no savings, and live from month to month, what happens if there are emergency expenses? You would need to take out a loan and enter into debt. Savings protect from having to borrow for necessary purchases, such as a washing machine, car repairs or other unexpected necessities. Counsellors recommend an emergency funs of around 1000 dollars for short-term emergencies or, much better, a reserve of three to six months living expenses to see you through loss of income through unemployment or sickness

7.   DISCARD CREDIT CARDS.

If financial problems crop up due to easy overspending with credit cards, it would be wise to cut them up! Practice plastic surgery! I personally use a credit card for traveling and ease of purchase, using their built-in insurance, but I would recommend not having credit cards if you are prone to impulse buying, if you already have excessive amounts of consumer debt, or if you cannot pay off the balance each month.

8.   RESIST IMPULSE BUYING.

A lot of purchases are made on-the-spot. I like to use a 24-hour rule, which forces me to wait and evaluate if I really need the item before buying it. Also, making a shopping list before going to the store is a help to avoid impulse buying.
High priced items, such as a car, boat, or house, should never be bought on impulse.

9.   SHARE, LEND, BORROW.

Part of our love affair with shopping and consumerism is because we think we need to personally own everything. In our neighborhood, we have an app in which tools and other items can be shared. This is not only good economic sense but also serves to build relationships.

Sharing honors God and wins friends. Borrowing something from someone, provided it is returned on time and in good shape and they are willing to lend, is a way to build and express gratitude. And it will save you money, especially on things you don't often use. Many websites stimulate lending and borrowing among neighbors. Doing this increases a community's closeness and effectiveness.

DAY 21: QUESTIONS TO PONDER

In what ways could you increase your financial margin to achieve faith financial goals?

How does this impact your thinking relative to long-term financial goals?

How does this impact your thinking relative to short-term financial goals?

DAY 22: MULTIPLYING RESOURCES

KEY VERSE

"He who supplies seed to the sower and bread for food will supply and multiply your seed for sowing and increase the harvest of your righteousness. You will be enriched in every way to be generous in every way, which through us will produce thanksgiving to God."

2 Corinthians 9:10-11

J esus said, "Lay up for yourselves treasures in heaven" (Matthew 6:20). Apparently, this treasure is for ourselves and therefore can be used by us.

We need to think of our "treasures in heaven" as an account with debits and credits. We can make deposits into this account, and we can withdraw from it. But despite some similarities, this is not the same as an earthly bank account: it is not subject to the economic restraints of earthly banks.

The economy of the world works by percentage increase. Banks pay interest at a very low percentage. The economy of the kingdom, however, works by multiplication. The parables Jesus told of the talents and the pounds deal at face value with stewardship of money while illustrating kingdom principles. In both parables, Jesus praised the servants who multiplied the money entrusted to them.

In the parable of Matthew 25 there was a multiplication by two; in the parable in Luke 19 there was a multiplication by five and by ten.

As Jesus sat in the Temple with His disciples watching people give money to the treasury, he said that many who were rich put in a lot. When a poor widow came and threw in two small coins, He said, "Truly, I tell you, this poor widow has put in more than all of them. For they all contributed out of their abundance, but she out of her poverty put in all she had to live on" (Luke 21:3-4).

I believe this widow understood the concept of storing up treasures in heaven – for herself. Having given all she had to live on, she must have had faith to believe that God's method of supply would come back to her. The earthly temple is modeled on the real one, which is in heaven itself (see Hebrews 9:24).
Jesus has now taken his place in heaven and is overseeing our account in the heavenly temple, just as he sat down in the earthly temple with his disciples to see how people deposited into it. The widow's story illustrates Jesus' teaching in Luke 6:38, "Give, and it will be given to you. Good measure, pressed down, shaken together, running over, will be put into your lap. For with the measure you use it will be measured back to you."

Jesus knew that the rich young man – if he had given away all he possessed – would need a source of future finances. And He also knew that the young man's wealth had a hold on him and that as long as it did, he would never be free to follow Jesus.
Paul instructed Timothy to teach people how to relate to their money. In 1 Timothy 6:17-19, Paul is warning people not to be proud or arrogant and not to set their hopes on uncertain riches but on God, who richly and without ceasing provides us with everything to enjoy. They ought to be rich in good works, generous, and ready to share. In this way they are "storing up treasure for themselves as a good foundation for the future so that they may take hold of that which is truly life."

Paul is teaching Timothy that we are to give when the Lord instructs us, and that this amount is credited to our heavenly account – unaffected by inflation, deflation, devaluation, or any other financial problems. This makes our heavenly account the only place in which our hearts can safely find rest and peace. Paul says that giving is a foundation for our future. Then we can grasp that which is life indeed!

In Philippians 4:17-19, Paul instructs believers about handling money. I like the explanation of this text by the writers of the Amplified Bible, who make it very clear how the finances of the kingdom of God should be considered. "Not that I seek the gift itself, but I do seek the profit which increases to your [heavenly] account [the blessing which is accumulating for you]." Giving opens up a debit and credit account in giving and receiving. The money the Philippians gave (debit) to Paul was not only to help Paul's ministry but also to accumulate (credit) to and multiply their own account. This is also a description of the "treasures in heaven." Paul knew they would need finances in the future and that by crediting the account in the present, there would be plenty in the account from which to withdraw in the future.

In the book of Acts we read the story of the Roman centurion Cornelius and his encounter with an angel of God who told him, "Your prayers and your generous] gifts to the poor have come up as a sacrifice] to God and have been remembered by Him" (Acts 10:4, AMPC). It appears that God kept a record of Cornelius's generosity.
I believe we can withdraw from this heavenly account even today. God responds to our faith: "Without faith it is impossible to please him" (Hebrews 11:6). If we ask for resources in the name of Jesus to be used in His way and for His purposes, they will be given. But we should not expect Him to release funds from the heavenly account to finance an ever-expanding lifestyle. Paul wrote, "God is able to make all grace abound to you, so that having all sufficiency in all things at all times, you may abound in every good work" (2 Corinthians 9:8). So we first have to determine in prayer what "all sufficiency" means – what is sufficient for us. How much is enough to live on given my current responsibilities? Then the Lord can release funds needed for "every good work."

Having said this, we should also note what the Macedonian believers did. Paul described this in 2 Corinthians 8:1-4. "We want you to know, brothers, about the grace of God that has been given among the churches of Macedonia, for in a severe test of affliction, their abundance of joy and their extreme poverty have overflowed

in a wealth of generosity on their part. For they gave according to their means, as I can testify, and beyond their means, of their own accord, begging us earnestly for the favor of taking part in the relief of the saints."
We may be called to give way beyond our means by "the grace of God."

PRIMING THE PUMP

 The following letter was found in a baking-powder can wired to the handle of an old pump that offered the only hope of drinking water on a very long and seldom-used trail across Nevada's Amargosa Desert. [51] A withered old cowboy named Desert Pete wrote:
"This pump is all right as of June 1932. I put a new sucker washer into it and it ought to last five years. But the washer dries out and the pump has got to be primed. Under the white rock I buried a bottle of water, out of the sun and cork end up. There's enough water in it to prime the pump, but not if you drink some first. Pour about one-fourth and let her soak to wet the leather. Then pour in the rest medium fast and pump like crazy. You'll git water. The well has never run dry. Have faith.
When you git watered up, fill the bottle and put it back like you found it for the next feller.
P.S. Don't go drinking the water first. Prime the pump with it and you'll git all you can hold."

A good example of priming the pump is Elijah's visit to a widow in Zarephath in the middle of an extreme drought. He asked her for some water and bread. The widow replied that she had nothing but a handful of flour and some oil that she was about to make for herself and her son, expecting then to die.
Elijah said, "Don't worry, make the bread and bring some to me first, then eat yourselves." He then went on to promise that the Lord would provide for her. "'The jar of flour shall not be spent, and the jug of oil shall not be empty, until the day that the LORD sends rain upon the earth.' And she went and did as Elijah said. And she and he and her household ate for many days."

She made an investment in God's plan and experienced multiplication of her resources (see 1 Kings 17:8-17).

FIVE USES OF MONEY

 "He who supplies seed to the sower and bread for food will supply and multiply your seed for sowing and increase the harvest of your righteousness" (2 Corinthians 9:10). Paul explains the purpose of this multiplication in the next sentence. "You will be enriched in every way to be generous in every way, which through us will produce thanksgiving to God" (2 Corinthians 9:11).
We can see here five biblical uses of money.

1. SEED FOR SOWING

I believe this seed to be sown is the tithe, which is the first ten percent of our harvest. In the case of salaried employees, this is calculated on gross income before taxes. If you are
a business owner, the tithe should be on the profits of the business. The Bible is very clear that the first part belongs to God, not the government. In my country, The Netherlands, the government allows charitable giving up to ten percent of our income to be deducted before tax is paid. This is the government recognizing that the first part belongs to God!
I believe that the tithe should be part of our financial circle, apportioning the firstfruits to God each month.

Dedicating the tithe to God is not giving – it is returning to the Lord what rightfully belongs to Him! It is not a formula for blessing, prosperity, an answer to financial problems, or improved standing with God. It is obedience to the word of God and an acknowledgement that He is our Lord and the owner of everything.
Dedicating the tithe to God contributes to a strong heart relationship with God. Remember Jesus' words, *"For where your treasure is, there your heart will be also"* (Matthew 6:21).

Dedicating the tithe to God moves money into the kingdom of God, where it can be multiplied in God's fields. *"Bring the full tithe into the storehouse, that there may be food in my house.*
And thereby put me to the test, says the LORD of hosts, if I will not open the windows of heaven for you and pour down for you a blessing until there is no more need" (Malachi 3:10). I believe the "storehouse" means the family household of God, or the local fellowship to whom you belong.

2. BREAD FOR FOOD

This concerns money spent for our personal needs. Because God is our provider, we can be assured that our needs
will be met. We have already discussed the importance of determining how much is enough for myself and my family. The way to find our answer and practice this is to "close our financial circle."
The purpose is not to spend as much as we can on ourselves but to determine reasonable amounts for our daily sustenance (bread for food), and to use the rest to be generous and forward God's interests.
God's heart is to bless us and provide financially for His calling and purposes to be fulfilled in our lives. If our circle is not closed, I am convinced that God will not provide financial increase to be spent on our ever-increasing lifestyle: we would likely consume His increase, and the word "consume" basically means to destroy!

3. MULTIPLICATION OF SEED

As we limit our living expenses by closing our circle, God can provide us with more than we need, producing overflow that can be invested, or "sown" into God's kingdom with the deliberate intention of reaping a kingdom harvest. Money for this multiplication comes initially from the overflow of our closed circle. "The point is this: whoever sows sparingly will also reap sparingly, and whoever sows bountifully will also reap bountifully" (2 Corinthians 9:6). Depositing our tithes and offerings into a "kingdom account" allows God to multiply this account and release finances for the advancement of the kingdom. The kingdom has its own investment system, called "sowing and reaping." All funds contributed into these kingdom accounts go directly toward the advancement of the kingdom to multiply followers and disciples of Jesus.

I believe that investing with a view to reaping these kingdom benefits is meant for our personal ministry calling, for projects in which we are involved. It should also be accompanied by prayer to water and feed the soil, asking for God's blessing.
One more thing: project investments should be placed in good soil. This necessitates our best efforts to evaluate the soil's fruit-bearing capacity and amend it for optimum fertility. Obviously, God plays a role in this, but we also carry ongoing responsibility to use the experience and growing wisdom He grants us (see Mark 4).

4. INCREASING THE FRUITS OF RIGHTEOUSNESS

Fruit comes forth from its seed. We transfer the seed of money via tithes and gifts into God's kingdom. This money is not for ourselves: we have already been taken care of in the previous section.
We use this money God gives us for the two highest purposes – as given in the two great commandments – to love God with all our heart and love others as ourselves. We also use it to combat unrighteousness in society. We can help people out of slavery to debt; we can help the poor, orphans, and widows.
God's major goal is to gather people *"from all nations, tribes and tongues"* and prepare for Jesus a Bride, the body of believers. Proverbs 11:30 states, *"The fruit of the righteous is a tree of life, and whoever captures souls is wise."* The tree of life will bring forth the fruit of the Spirit, which will overflow in us (see Part 2 of this book), and the fruit of reproduction as we make new disciples.

5. GENEROSITY

I believe that biblical generosity is different from the tithe, which belongs to God. Generosity comes out of our offerings, giving as the Lord directs and without the expectation of anything in return. The nature of an offering is that it is not an obligation but a freely given sacrifice that costs us something. Tithes are returned to the Owner. Offerings are given as signs of love and thankfulness.

"Do not neglect to do good and to share what you have, for such sacrifices are pleasing to God" (Hebrews 13:16).

King David, in his preparations for the building of the temple, was able to gather a great offering from the people. He was amazed at this outpouring of generosity, realizing in his prayer that they were able to give because God first gave for them to be able to give.

"But who am I, and what is my people, that we should be able thus to offer willingly? For all things come from you, and of your own have we given you" (1 Chronicles 29:14).

My friend Albert Diepeveen always said, "You cannot outgive God. Whatever you give He gives back in order for us to give more." We can give because God first of all gave to us. You can never outgive God. He is looking for people who have closed their circles, so that he can allow finances to overflow for

His purposes.

All the five purposes together result in thanksgiving to God.

MULTIPLYING THE RESOURCES GOD GIVES US

The economy of God's kingdom works by multiplication, not addition.

A first illustration is our agricultural economy. If a sower sows seeds in well-worked soil, he would not expect to receive

a small percentage increase. The seeds multiply and the yields as expressed in the parable of the sower are *"some a hundredfold, some sixty, some thirty"* (Matthew 13:8). An

investment of one would come back to return a hundred, sixty, or thirty times more!

We all, having been made in the image of God – believers or not – have notions of eternity hardwired into our being. We also have this inner feeling that everything we do should be multiplied; we

tend to be dissatisfied when it doesn't happen that way. That's why people gamble in the lottery or
casinos and take huge risks with financial products of dubious morality: they think their investments should give a much greater return than money normally yields in a "safe" economy.
But only one economy is truly safe. Only that which is invested in what God has created and blessed is sure to be multiplied
– whether it is human creativity and ideas, products, people, righteousness, or yes, even money. The requirement is that these are invested in the kingdom of God for His purposes.
God will multiply whatever we place into His hands by faith.

It was late in the day. For hours Jesus had held an audience captive with his unique style of teaching and obvious authority. John 6:1-14 and Matthew 14:13-21 tell what happens when the disciples realize that the crowd must also be physically hungry. They ask Jesus to send the crowd away to get food for themselves. Jesus gives them this startling challenge: "You feed them!"
Faced with an insurmountable challenge to their budget, they calculate the deficit. "Two hundred denarii (a denarii was pay for a day's work) worth of bread would not be enough for each of them to get a little."
However, a small boy came with the equivalent of a Hebrew Happy Meal. The boy gave what he intended for his own consumption. When placed in the hands of the disciples, with Jesus' blessing and power, the fish sandwiches multiplied to feed thousands with more left over than they started with.

When do think the multiplication exactly happened? It started when the disciples distributed the bread to the people. They did the actual multiplying of what a small boy had provided, and Jesus had commanded, similar to the oil which had multiplied to solve a widow's financial problems. When you're a disciple and Jesus blesses what you have in your hands, your efforts are multiplied. Walter Bruegemann stated, "In feeding the hungry crowd, Jesus reminds us that the wounds of scarcity can be healed only by faith in God's promise of abundance." [52]

DAY 22: QUESTIONS TO PONDER

203

Jot down your thoughts on the five biblical uses of money:

1. Seed for sowing

2. Bread for food

3. Multiplication of seed

4. Increasing the fruits of righteousness

5. Generosity

DAY 23: FINANCIAL FINISH LINES

KEY VERSE

"But God said to him, 'Fool! This night your soul is required of you, and the things you have prepared, whose will they be?' So is the one who lays up treasure for himself and is not rich toward God."

Luke 12:20-21

A finish line helps determine when we have finished the race. I encourage you to set a finish line for your income and wealth accumulation and cap your spending accumulation at a pre-determined point. As your wealth increases, the endless ways to spend it also increases.

Our consumer culture promotes one overarching goal: The accumulation of more and more. We are endlessly told that we need a bigger house, a newer car, a nicer vacation, more money in savings, and on it goes.

A small but growing number of Christians are declaring that they don't need more.

They have stated what is enough and drawn a 'financial finish line.' Could I be content with food and clothing that are enough for just today, as Paul admonishes Timothy? "But if we have food and clothing, with these we will be content." (1 Timothy 6:8) Could I go on a spending freeze instead of a spending frenzy?

How much is enough? How much do I need to accumulate to reach my long-term goals, such as retirement, education, inheritance, business goals? Could I be content with food and clothing that are enough for just today? Could I go on a spending freeze instead of a spending frenzy? How much is enough for long- term goals, retirement, education, inheritance, business, etc.?

REASONS FOR A FINISH LINE

 Imagine athletes lining up for a race without an agreed, clear finish line. Are we running a 100-meter dash, or a marathon? If we know the finish line, we can pace ourselves, knowing when to speed up and when to slow down. When we reach the line, we can stop, and take stock.
A financial finish line is that stage of your financial growth at which you don't have to accumulate any more. Your financial finish line is the answer to an all-important question: "How much is enough?" Here are some reasons why it is prudent to set a financial finish line..

A FINISH LINE PROVIDES DIRECTION

Without a finish line, you won't know how much you need to accumulate, how much to invest, and when you reach your goal. If you have a clear view of your destination, the goals you want to achieve, then setting out a strategy to reach that destination is much easier. If you aim at nothing, you will it that every time. You will be able to periodically evaluate if you are on track or lagging behind.

A FINISH LINE TELLS US WHEN WE'VE ARRIVED

The best part of racing is crossing the finishing line. It gives us a sense of satisfaction and achievement. We can then sit back a while and ponder.
To run a race successfully, it is necessary to keep our eyes on the finish line and not get distracted. Without a finish line, we will never know when we arrived anywhere. Financially, we could never realise what 'enough' is. Without a finish line, we don't really know where we are heading.

A FINISH LINE HELPS US TO BE CONTENT

 A finishing line will help us to commit to a lifestyle of becoming content with what we have and spending less, so that we can save more for future goals.

If we set our financial faith goals in prayer, agreeing with God what these should be, then we can rest knowing that the Lord will guide us and keep us content and thankful, no matter what the outcome. We can keep the finish line in view, but remain flexible and open to the Lord's guidance.

Contentment doesn't come from accumulating more but from desiring less. When you set a financial finish line, you have answered the question of how much is enough?

Setting and achieving the finish line is not the same as finishing well: it's a precursor. The finish line is a milestone within your plan to finish well. Setting a finish line positions you to finish well and helps you to stay on track in your financial Jesus warns us to be careful not to allow a spirit of greed to invade our wealth growth, but to be 'rich toward God,' employing our wealth to practically love God and our neighbor. That is the standard by which we shall be judged.

Jesus' parable of the rich fool causes us to consider exactly how much we will really need to save in order to achieve our God-given goals. He teaches us about the danger of crossing a line of enough into greed at the expense of generosity..

To avoid blindly saving with no limits, building bigger barns.), set financial finish lines for each strategic goal, making a financial plan to know how much I will need to reach specific goals. This protects me from striving for a false security and leaves more room for giving.

TWO FINISH LINES

In the book, *God and Money: How We Discovered True Riches at Harvard Business School,* authors Gregory Baumer and John Cortines propose the principle of financial finish lines as a powerful weapon in the battle to answer the question, How much is enough? They recommend establishing two financial finish lines: a spending finish line and a wealth finish line. Of course, to avoid the "just a little bit more" trap, these finish lines must be established well before you reach them. [53]

The first finish line is the spending finish line, where you establish a limit on how much you will spend on daily living. The figures may need to be adjusted for major life events such as unemployment, marriage, or kids. We
discussed the concept of establishing your financial circle as a tool to help you establish this spending finish line in Day 20.

The second finish line is a wealth finish line. The amount of your finish line is a personal choice. Up until now this plan is not much different than a lot of the "Retire by age …" plans that are so common.

The difference happens after you reach your wealth finish line. Instead of retiring, you keep working – but now you give all your additional income away, like Toby Ord and his
club are doing. I love this idea of financial finish lines with the extra devoted to giving. What a great way to add happiness, meaning, and fun to the later part of your working years and into retirement.

Reaching your wealth finish line also provides freedom. If you love what you are doing, you might choose to just keep doing it, but crossing the wealth finish line gives you other options. You could try a different type of work or simply work less and use some of your extra time to help others.

The key is to establish the two finish lines in advance and stick to them. The goal is to get off the treadmill: to win the battle of "more vs. enough" and move on to the more important work of fulfilling God's plans for your life.

BIGGER BARNS?

The parable of the Rich Fool (Luke 12:16-21) gives us an example of someone who ignored his finish line and continued accumulating. The farmer tore down his barns and built bigger ones. Jesus warns is through this parable that those who never stop accumulating are greedy and foolish as they "lay treasures up for themselves," and are not "rich towards God."
The other element in the story relates to the potential implications of retirement and God's view on multiplication as a journey rather than a destination. In the story, part of the issue Jesus had with the rich fool could have been that he simply stopped. His idea of a finish line was a simple thought: *my work is done, it's time to relax and enjoy life to the full.*
Judging by his outcome, we can clearly conclude that God desires something better for us and expects something better from us as financial disciples rather than rich fools. *"But God said to him, 'Fool! This night your soul is required of you, and the things you have prepared, whose will they be?'"* (Luke 12:20).
Be sure not to confuse earthly concepts like retirement with eternal concepts like fulfilling the Great Commission. That work never stops! The expectation Jesus has for us is to make disciples, right up to the day we meet Him.

The parable of the rich fool tells us that the farmer was already rich when a season of abundance came. God called him a fool when he "thought to himself" that he would tear down his existing barns and build newer, bigger ones. God was not angry that the farmer was rich. He called the farmer a fool because of his attitude. He said to himself, "Soul, you have ample goods laid up for many years; relax, eat, drink, be merry." (verse 19),
God does not want us to store up things for ourselves; rather, He expects us to be rich toward Him, to experience true wealth. "So is the one who lays up treasure for himself and is not rich toward God" (verse 21). The rich fool had a distorted view of financial independence. To be financially independent for the farmer was to be dependent on money and independent from God. True

financial independence means to be fully and completely dependent on the Lord!

He was oblivious of the fact that wealth is a blessing from God. "The blessing of the LORD makes rich, and he adds no sorrow with it." (Proverbs 10;22) He did not realize that wealth should be shared to meet the needs of those around him. He was engrossed with himself. Five times he says "I …"
He did not realize that he would be held accountable to the One who had given him life.
When I die, I don't want to leave behind a large sum of money in the bank.
My ultimate goal is to use as much wealth as possible to advance the cause of God's kingdom during my lifetime.

HOW DO YOU DEFINE A BARN?

So what exactly constitutes your "barn," in financial terms? A barn is a fixed structure. It is planned for and built to exact specifications once; then it doesn't change. It holds a certain amount of grain based on those specifications. It can hold less but it can't hold more. It has a clear purpose – to store grain, usually for the short-term, when the grain is then moved to create value in other ways (e.g., to make cereal or tortillas).

Barn building means accumulating wealth. Without any specific God-given goals for investing surplus cash to build wealth, it can quickly become a kind of idol in which we trust for provision of what we need.
We need to plan intentionally to meet our needs and remain vigilant that accumulating does not become hoarding.
According to a definition in Wikipedia, hoarding is a mental disorder characterized by accumulation of possessions due to excessive acquisition of or difficulty discarding them, regardless of their actual value, leading to clinically significant distress or impairment in personal, family, social, educational, occupational or other important areas of functioning. [10]

The farmer demonstrated this mental disorder, as it was clearly diagnosed by God.   Having proudly talked to his soul about his achievement, God called him a fool.
Building barns is fine to save wealth for future goals which have been planned together with God in prayer.

HOW TO SET A FINANCIAL FINISH LINE

 Our first step is, of course. To sit down with our spouse, if married, and spend time discussing our future need with each other and with God, in prayer. Many people do this during a 'financial retreat' over a few days with the specific purpose of discovering God's plan for their lives, and what financial consequences that plan brings with it. Define your goals in financial terms as best you can and start saving!

Basically, you can only set your faith financial goals in six areas. Paying long-term debt, such as your mortgage or business loans. Ensuring you can meet college costs for your children. I set finish lines for my children's education and am now saving towards the education of my grandchildren, not wanting them to get into debt. Other long-term goals could be your retirement, leaving a legacy and lastly, starting a business, or helping others start a business. I once saved to help start a business in Cairo, Egypt to help a missionary establish himself there.

MAKING IT TO THE FINISH LINE

Derek Redmond of Great Britain popped his hamstring in the 1992 Olympic 400-meter semi-final. He limped painfully towards the finish. His father, Jim
Redmond, couldn't just watch his son limping in such pain. He rushed down to the track, put his arms around his son and they struggled together for over a hundred meters to the finish line. [11]

Together they made the finish line! It will be very helpful to involve others into our journey. Some family member, friends and advisors will be needed to help us along the way and make sure we don't make silly mistakes or get into the danger of hoarding. We, in turn, can help others to reach their financial finish lines by being available to help them focus on God's goals for them, applying Biblical principles for investing, saving and spending and generally following Jesus in their financial life.

DAY 23: QUESTIONS TO PONDER

How would you apply the principle of a finish line to the rich hoarder in Luke 12?

How would you define a financial "barn"?

What does setting a finish line mean to you, practically?

DAY 24: FINANCING THE KINGDOM

KEY VERSE

"And I tell you, make friends for yourselves by means of unrighteous wealth, so that when it fails they may receive you into the eternal dwellings."

Luke 16:9

Long ago, trappers found the best way to catch a monkey: take a jar with a narrow neck, put a fig inside, and then put the jar inside a cage. The monkey would come along, reach inside the cage, and put his hand into the jar to grab the fig. When he tried to pull his hand out, it wouldn't fit through the narrow neck unless he let go of the fig – which he refused to do. He was trapped on the outside of the cage because the jar wouldn't fit through the bars!

It's the same with us. If we hold on to our money with a closed fist, it traps us. It becomes our focus, our sense of identity, our worth. Only when we open our hands and loosen our grip will we become free. I constantly ask myself, Are my hands open or closed?

IRRESPONSIBLE GENEROSITY

Jesus' life mission is recorded as: "For even the Son of Man came not to be served but to serve, and to give his life as a ransom for many" (Mark 10:45). The ultimate goal is to spend as much as you can for your friends to enjoy eternity with God and "receive you into the eternal dwellings" (Luke 16:9).

This reflects an important and essential ingredient of financial discipleship: using money for what the world views as uneconomic purposes: helping people focus on God and His eternal plans. This can be done by giving the firstfruits of our income and making sacrifices. Money given to the church, to evangelism, to widows and orphans, and to the poor is placed outside of the normal economic circuit. As we have emphasized, our global economy is measured by buying and selling. The economy of God's kingdom is measured by giving and receiving.

A characteristic of the Church's distinctive ethic is its generosity that transcends scarcity.
One of the basic economic teachings we learn in college is the allocation of scarce resources. There is only so much to go around: a piece of property cannot be enjoyed by everyone.
A certain sum of money can satisfy only a limited number of desires. But the principles of the kingdom transcend and defy the complex theories of our world's economists. A poor widow who gives her last two small copper coins, all she has left,
is said to have offered more than all the rich combined. The Corinthian church's "extreme poverty" overflows into a "wealth of generosity" that turns out to be an "abundance" that supplies the needs of others (2 Corinthians 8:2,14).
By worldly standards, these Corinthians would seem to lack financial responsibility in being cheerfully generous "beyond their means" (2 Corinthians 8:3).

The actual amount we give is not the most important thing. Let me appeal once again to the story of how Jesus "sat down opposite the treasury and watched the people putting money into the offering box. Many rich people put in large sums. And
a poor widow came and put in two small copper coins." Jesus was teaching His disciples an important lesson. "Truly, I say to you, this poor widow has put in more than all those who are contributing to the offering box. For they all contributed out of their abundance, but she out of her poverty has put in everything she had, all she had to live on" (Mark 12:41-44). By worldly standards this is irresponsible.
Did she then go home in despair and suffer starvation? I believe not. She was convinced that God would provide for her.

When analyzed by economic rules, this all seems irrational. But God's economy thrives as He multiplies that which we put into His hands. He is "able to make all grace abound to you, so that having all sufficiency in all things at all times, you may abound in every good work" (2 Corinthians 9:8). When the impoverished give generously, God makes them "enriched in every way to be generous in every way" (2 Corinthians 9:11).

This seemingly irresponsible generosity makes everyone spiritually richer in ways that economists can never calculate. "This service that you perform is not only supplying the needs of the Lord's people but is also overflowing in many expressions of thanks to God. Because of the service by which you have proved yourselves, others will praise God for the obedience that accompanies your confession of the gospel of Christ, and for your generosity in sharing with them and with everyone else. And in their prayers for you, their hearts will go out to you, because of the surpassing grace God has given you" (2 Corinthians 9:12-14).

The God who owns "the cattle on a thousand hills" (Psalm 50:10) and the gold in every mine (Haggai 2:8) can easily defy the laws of human economics!

The great evangelist Dwight Moody used to tell a story of a farmer, known for his stinginess, who came to faith. A neighbor in distress came to him for help. The farmer, now eager to demonstrate the genuineness of his faith, decided to give the neighbor a ham. But then he began to have second thoughts, and the tempter whispered to him, "Give him the smallest one you have; you can't really afford it." Struggling with his conscience, he took the largest ham he had. "You fool!" the tempter said.
The farmer replied, "Shut up, if you don't keep quiet, I'll give him every ham in the smokehouse!" [54]

RELEASING RESOURCES FOR KINGDOM WORK

 Back in 2007, we wanted to start a ministry to help people out of debt. One out of every five households in the Netherlands was suffering from over-indebtedness with accompanying symptoms like poverty, suicide, mental problems, and marriage breakdown. To drive the ministry, we wanted to hire a full-time leader. We had no money, but we knew that it was high in God's priorities to set people free.
After prayer, a few business guys put together a small fund of about 50,000 euros, just enough to pay someone for six months. We believed that in sowing this money into the field of God's kingdom, He could multiply it to establish the ministry.
We started the work, helping people along the road to freedom. At the end of the six-month period, we received a grant from the Dutch government for two million euros to be spent on the project. I really believe that our seed money was multiplied in the kingdom and released for a project that met the Lord's approval.

As I write, tens of thousands of people are being helped each year, and many are finding Christ as a result.

I believe this is a pattern for releasing funds for kingdom work. It can be illustrated as follows.

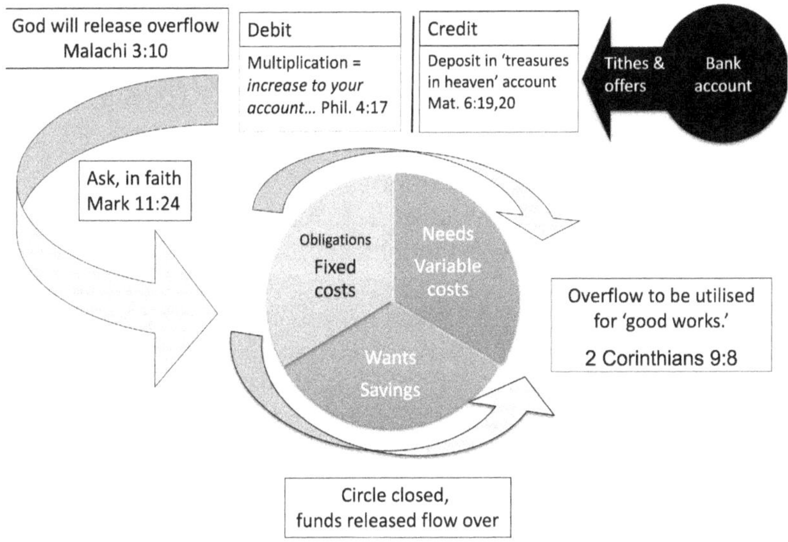

The starting point is sowing into the kingdom of God through tithes and offerings. I use the word "sowing" on purpose. When we sow seed, we expect a return; we expect that the seed will be multiplied. I call this sowing into my "treasures in heaven" account. Jesus commanded us to lay up for ourselves "treasures in heaven" (Matthew 6:20). Paul encouraged Timothy to teach people with excess funds to invest in the kingdom. "They are to do good, to be rich in good works, to be generous and ready to share, thus storing up treasure for themselves as a good foundation for the future, so that they may take hold of that which is truly life" (1 Timothy 6:18-19). Those who share generously are "storing up treasure for themselves... "

Note that this storing of treasure is for ourselves, the sharers! As followers of Jesus, our heart is to extend His lordship over all, making it our desire to use our stored treasure for kingdom purposes.

When we store money in our "treasures in heaven" account, this gets multiplied in God's economy. Far beyond a mere percentage increase as with a worldly investment, God will take our seed and actually multiply it. Paul said to the generous believers in Philippi, "Not that I seek the gift, but I seek the fruit that increases to your credit" (Philippians 4:17).

Just as earthly accounts are designed for flows both in and out, our kingdom account is set up for us to make good-faith withdrawals. This means trusting the Lord to provide what is needed, agreeing with Him for the purpose of the funds, and using the monies in His way. "Therefore I tell you, whatever you ask in prayer, believe that you have received it, and it will be yours" (Mark 11:24).

When the Lord releases funds from our *"treasures in heaven"* account, we must guard against using them for our own consumption. I believe this conflict of interest doesn't resolve until we have closed our circle and have defined what is enough. Although Jesus and Paul told us to lay up treasures for ourselves, this does not mean funding an ever-increasing lifestyle. Funds will only be released when they flow over into kingdom use.

THREE GIVING GOALS

 Three key Scripture passages have helped me define my call to serve the world in the name of Christ. I'll give each, followed by an example of its outworking in my experience.

First, Jesus famously launched His ministry in Luke 4:18-19. *"The Spirit of the Lord is upon me, because he has anointed me to proclaim good news to the poor. He has sent me to proclaim liberty to the captives and recovering of sight to the blind, to set at liberty those who are oppressed, to proclaim the year of the Lord's favor."*

Jesus had a clear focus on reaching people with deep and desperate needs.

One of my favorite ministry investments is the national project I described earlier: helping tens of thousands of people get out of financial debt and setting many free from spiritual bondage as well. This is using *"unrighteous wealth"* in a righteous way – to populate *"the eternal dwellings"* (Luke 16:9).

Second, Paul writes in 2 Corinthians 5:18, "All this is from God, who through Christ reconciled us to himself and gave us the ministry of reconciliation." This ministry of reconciliation is to spread the gospel, telling people that they can be reconciled to God through the work of Jesus on the cross.

I have been a member of a Christian businessmen's group for over thirty years. Our main focus was to introduce business and professional people to Christ. Our strategy was to invite business associates to a meal in a restaurant or hotel at which a Christian businessperson would give their testimony and invite people to know Jesus. I brought guests and paid for their meal – a wonderful investment. Giving to movements that bring the gospel to people yields eternal fruit!

Finally, Jesus left His followers with the Great Commission before He ascended to heaven. Matthew 28:19-20 states, "Go therefore and make disciples of all nations, baptizing them in the name of the Father and of the Son and of the Holy Spirit, teaching them to observe all that I have commanded you. . ."

I have been involved in a disciple-making ministry since 1970, investing money in these movements that help people know Christ more intimately and grow into mature Christians who can help others do the same. I have seen that investing in discipleship ministries produces leaders who go on to help others find and follow Christ.

INVESTING IN PEOPLE

Earlier, I recalled a story Jesus told in Luke 16, about a business manager who did his creditors a favor by releasing a considerable part of what they owed. His motivation was to introduce these creditors to grace in the hope that they might return the favor. His boss commended him for being shrewd. In verse 9, Jesus explains the reason He told the story. *"And I tell you,*

make friends for yourselves by means of unrighteous wealth, so that when it fails they may receive you into the eternal dwellings."
Making "friends" referred to patron-client relationships in the Greco-Roman world in which economic and social benefits were traded. This was seen simply as an unavoidable social reality in the same way that purchasing goods with money cannot be avoided in our time.
The manager made "friends" in order to be repaid with social benefits, whereas throughout Luke's Gospel, Jesus teaches that making "friends" is to be done without hope of reciprocation. *"Give to everyone who begs from you, and from one who takes away your goods does not demand them back"* (Luke 6:30). *"But love your enemies, and do good, and lend, expecting nothing in return, and your reward will be great"* (Luke 6:35).
Jesus calls us to genuinely make friends with those who cannot repay us, thus creating social unity between rich and poor.

It is these acts of compassion that have a bearing on our ultimate judgement – *"make friends for yourselves by means of unrighteous wealth, so that when it fails they may receive you into the eternal dwellings."*
Jesus is asking us to use the money given to us in trust by God to preach the gospel and make disciples. These people will become your friends. They will have much in common with you, and when you get to heaven, your *"eternal dwelling,"* they will be there to welcome you. That will give you immense joy!

A key question to ask is, What will be in heaven? Although much of this is beyond our imagination, one thing we know is that people will be there. This makes it obvious that one way we *"lay up treasures in heaven"* is to invest in the lives of people. This is the kind of investment we will indeed take with us. Money invested in people is the best possible investment.
The proper use of money is not for living high down here: that would be a very poor investment indeed. Of course, we need to keep a certain amount of money to carry on the day-to-day business of life, but we want to free up as much as we can in order to place it where the return is eternal.

This is a kind of born-again stewardship, using what has been entrusted to you exactly as the Master desires – for His eternal goals. This is the essence of financial discipleship.

The problem with much stewardship teaching it is that is so me-centered. Most books and courses on stewardship deal with managing your personal finances. That's okay, of course, but it is not all. Stewardship also has to be good management of your time and relationships. Are you also stewarding the gospel – the good news that Jesus came to live in people and make them fit for eternity? Are you stewarding your relationships and your time to help people get to know Jesus and how to be good stewards themselves?

Everybody we make a friend by winning him or her for Jesus Christ is going to be a star in our crown in eternity. One of the best ways for me to spend money is to pay for someone to hear the gospel: buying lunch for a good chat, giving a book, or taking someone to a concert.

SCHINDLER'S LIST

Schindler's List is for me a very powerful film as it shows the developing life of an active Nazi who owned an Austrian factory. [55] In the beginning he manipulates Jewish people, using them for profit in his factory. After being influenced by the factory foreman and coming to his senses, he starts using all his assets in the factory to save the Jews working there, people who would otherwise be destined for the gas chambers. A scene at the end of this film is – at least for me

– the ultimate illustration of investing in people: setting them free to be all God wants them to be.

The scene occurs in the 1940s, toward the end of the war at a factory in Poland. German businessman Oscar Schindler has employed 1100 Polish Jews in his factory, thus sparing them from probable death in Auschwitz. While anticipating

liberation, the Jews saved by Schindler – among them his own accountant, Itzhak Stern – present him with a ring in gratitude. It is inscribed with a powerful statement. "It's Hebrew, from the Talmud," Stern explains. "It says 'Whoever saves one life saves the world entire.'"

 One of the final scenes unfolds as Schindler looks back on what he could have done to save more lives. Listen to the exchange between Schindler and Stern.
Oskar Schindler: "I could have got more out. I could have got more. I don't know. If I'd just… I could have got more."
Itzhak Stern: "Oskar, there are eleven hundred people who are alive because of you. Look at them."
Oskar Schindler: "If I'd made more money… I threw away so much money. You have no idea. If I'd just…"
Itzhak Stern: "There will be generations because of what you did."
Oskar Schindler: "I didn't do enough!" Itzhak Stern: "You did so much." Schindler looks at his car.
Oskar Schindler: "This car. Goeth would have bought this car. Why did I keep the car? Ten people right there. Ten people. Ten more people. [removing Nazi pin from lapel] This pin. Two people. This is gold. Two more people. He would have given me two for it, at least one. One more person. A person, Stern. For this. [sobbing] I could have gotten one more person… and I didn't! And I… I didn't!"
Itzhak replies, "Oskar, there are 1,100 people who are alive because of you. Look at them."
Oskar Schindler started the war in a bad way. He finished the war well.

After the war, he could not find any business success but was looked after by the so-called "Schindler Jews." He died penniless and was buried on Mount Zion in Jerusalem.
I consider the ultimate investment to be investing in people. Jesus said, "And I tell you, make friends for yourselves by means of unrighteous wealth, so that when it fails they may receive you into the eternal dwellings" (Luke 16:9).

DAY 24: QUESTIONS TO PONDER

225

After reading the three giving goals, what verses would you use to help you define your calling and giving goals?

What has using money to "make friends" looked like on your financial discipleship journey?

Who is somebody you haven't invested in yet that could be your "one more"?

PART 4: MAKING FINANCIAL DISCIPLES

DAY 25: FINANCIAL DISCIPLES

KEY VERSE

"For where your treasure is, there your heart will be also."

Matthew 6:21

A disciple is a person who has an ongoing, transformative relationship with Jesus Christ and happily shares what he or she has learned with others. A disciple has three primary tasks in life: follow Jesus, make disciples, and glorify God. You are probably wondering … Why financial disciples?

Jesus wants a love relationship with us. He stated that *"where your treasure is, there your heart will be also"* (Matthew 6:21).
Therefore, it is important to manage our "treasure," our finances, to make sure that they are dedicated to serving Him, because that will determine the focus and attention of our heart.
Loren Cunningham stated, "Money acts like a chameleon: it takes on the color of the owner's heart."

The way we spend our money is a direct reflection of our heart's priorities. It cannot be faked: it's recorded clearly in black and white on our bank statements. G. K. Chesterton once said, "Show me the stubs in a man's checkbook and I will tell you what kind of man he is." [56] Billy Graham put it a little differently: "Give me five minutes with a person's checkbook, and I will tell you where their heart is." [57] Most people don't have a checkbook anymore, but you get the idea.

Money is one way that our priorities and values are made visible. Godfrey Davis, who wrote a biography about the Duke of Wellington, said, "I found an old account ledger that showed how the duke spent his money. It was a far better clue to what he thought was really important than the reading of his letters or speeches." [58]

What we invest in is presumably what's most important in our lives. Jesus is concerned about our heart, the center of our being, and the fruit that the Spirit causes to spring out of our hearts. Money is not fruit, but the way we use our money should be an expression of the fruit of the Spirit. That's why financial discipleship is so important.

It is said that finances are the funny bone of discipleship. A funny bone is a part of the elbow over which a sensitive nerve passes. If the elbow is knocked on a hard table or door, you can experience a shock of pain, tingling, and numbness. The pain can radiate along the whole arm into the fingers. Actually, there's nothing funny about it! But the point is that our finances are also very sensitive, able to cause surprising discomfort.

Financial discipleship is central to our walk with Christ in this fallen world where money competes so directly with the Lord for priority in our hearts.

WHY TALK ABOUT BIBLICAL FINANCE IN CHURCH?

Money is a huge day-to-day issue in the lives of most people. Many spend a majority of their waking hours making money, spending money, worrying about money, fighting over money, or trying to protect their money. Alarming statistics tell the story of rapidly increasing consumer debt, saving rates that have fallen off a cliff, and conflict about money being a leading cause of divorce. Do you realize that one in six church families have problematic debt? Research suggests that more than a third of us are anxious about how to pay the bills.

Money, like food, is one of those things we all think about every

day – and often the thoughts cause anxiety resulting in stress. The most frequent questions are, Do I have enough? How much is enough? Will I ever have enough? How can
I get out of debt? Anxiety and uncertainty can lead to absence in church, lack of energy in church activities, and decreased giving.

THE TABOO

There is a strong reluctance to talk about money. It seems to be a very private matter – inappropriate for discussion, especially at church.
Yet the Bible gives clear warnings about what can happen when the topic of managing money is not addressed from a biblical perspective.
Very few Bible schools and theology courses devote any time to teaching about the handling of money and possessions.
That results in church leaders rarely having an intentional and structured understanding or approach to it beyond their teaching on giving.
People surely need a biblical framework and criteria for making financial decisions. Teaching them God's way is essential in the journey of discipleship.

Let's look at seven strong reasons why church leaders and pastors need to preach and teach a biblical perspective on our relationship to money and possessions:
1. Money is a major competitor for our devotion and seeks to divert us away from God. "No one can serve two masters. Either you will hate the one and love the other, or you will be devoted to the one and despise the other. You cannot serve both God and money" (Matthew 6:24, NIV).
2. Money problems choke the word and make it unfruitful as evidenced in the parable of the sower. "Still others, like seed sown among thorns, hear the word; but the worries of this life, the deceitfulness of wealth and the desires for other things come in and choke the word, making it unfruitful" (Mark 4: 18-19, NIV).

3. The way we use our money is an outside indicator of an inside spiritual state. *"For where your treasure is, there your heart will be also"* (Matthew 6:21, NIV).

4. The love of money lies at the root of all kinds of evil. "For the love of money is a root of all kinds of evil. Some people, eager for money, have wandered from the faith and pierced themselves with many griefs" (1 Timothy 6:10, NIV). Derek Prince, a well-known Bible teacher, commented on this verse: "In my teachings I often emphasized God's plan to bless the faithful especially in material things. But looking back I regret every opportunity where I propagated this message of prosperity without balancing it with Paul's warning."

5. Inability to pay back debt robs you of your freedom. *"Just as the rich rule the poor, so the borrower is servant to the lender"* (Proverbs 22:7, NLT).

6. The measure by which God entrusts to us His true riches is determined by the way we handle money. "Whoever can be trusted with very little can also be trusted with much, and whoever is dishonest with very little will also be dishonest with much. So if you have not been trustworthy in handling worldly wealth, who will trust you with true riches? And if you have not been trustworthy with someone else's property, who will give you property of your own?" (Luke 16:10-12, NIV).

7. And, in the words of the prophet, (Hosea 4:6, NLT), God's people were suffering because the priests failed to teach them God's ways. "My people are being destroyed because they don't know me. Since you priests refuse to know me, I refuse to recognize you as my priests. Since you have forgotten the laws of your God, I will forget to bless your children."

FINANCIAL DISCIPLESHIP

The Lord's commission to us is to *"Go and make disciples . . . teaching them to obey everything I have commanded you"* (Matthew 28:19-20, NIV). If we are not teaching people how to handle their finances God's way, then we are omitting a large part of His teaching. We need to preach, teach, and model financial discipleship.

Following Jesus in our financial life should be a major topic of learning for all believers. A Bible-based teaching program will have a huge impact on spiritual growth; it is an essential, if not critical, path of discipleship.

We need to make financial disciples due to the serious problems people are facing. These include:

1. Idolatry as we worship at the altar of materialism, bolstering ego and cluttering our lives with stuff we don't need and in many cases can't afford.
2. Materialism, leading to a lack of contentment and a restless existence, always being on the move for more and never experiencing true fulfillment.
3. Marriage tension and breakdown as couples fail to communicate about how to handle money issues.
4. Church budgets suffering and people not experiencing the joy of generosity because of a lack of giving.
5. Anxiety, lack of freedom, and strained relationships under the burden of debt.
6. Additional problems arising from gambling, stealing, cheating on taxes or expenses, and a variety of other negative behaviors the word teaches us to avoid.

When communicating God's truth about money and possessions, a general theme throughout is for people to gain *"the mind of Christ"* regarding their management of money and possessions. See 1 Corinthians 2 about our responsibility to teach God's wisdom as revealed by the Spirit.

Our culture is adrift with myths about money and its power and influence. We are led to confuse our self-worth with our net worth. The church may be the only remaining place where the issues can be discussed in non-market terms.

Today's pastors and leaders must be prepared to articulate, teach, train, and encourage their people toward a biblical perspective regarding money and possessions. The financial and spiritual well-being of many people are at stake.

THE ACRONYM D.I.S.C.I.P.L.E.

To describe a financial disciple, I use the acronym D.I.S.C.I.P.L.E

D – Decide to follow Jesus daily and take up our cross.

This means to follow the path Jesus took, which is the cross. There is no other starting point and no other way. *"Then he [Jesus] said to them all: 'Whoever wants to be my disciple must deny themselves and take up their cross daily and follow me'"* (Luke 9:23, NIV).
I love the hymn, "The Old Rugged Cross," written in 1912 by the evangelist and song leader George Bennard. [59] This gives me an accurate portrayal of the cross itself. Not a polished, jewel-adorned, silver cross but rough-hewn lumber with splinters – just like real life.

> O that old rugged cross, so despised by the world,
> Has a wondrous attraction for me;
> For the dear Lamb of God left his glory above
> To bear it to dark Calvary.
> So I'll cherish the old rugged cross,
> Till my trophies at last I lay down;
> I will cling to the old rugged cross,
> And exchange it some day for a crown.

Taking up the cross means to lay our trophies, our treasures, down until that day when we can exchange our cross for
a crown!

I – Identify with Jesus.

This means to anchor our identity in Christ and not in the world and its offerings. We need to realize that our worth is not in anything material or in any achievement but in the fact that we are beloved children of God.
When we meet Jesus at the cross and realize what he has done for us, all earthly gain or success, all prowess and skill pale into

insignificance compared to what he has done! Our worth is in Christ alone and He is our greatest treasure, lover of our soul, and fountain of all we will ever need.

Our culture leads us to define ourselves through our career, financial status, achievements, appearance, or popularity. Problems come when life is not going as we would like. We then try to derive our identity from belonging to a group of like-minded people. Or from buying certain possessions. These externals can never give us a stable sense of self because when circumstances change, our identity suffers.

When our identity is grounded in Christ, the first thing that comes to mind when we describe our status is someone deeply wanted and loved by God. We are valuable because of our Father, God Himself; because of what we cost, the
precious blood of Jesus; and because of what we can become as sons and daughters of the most high God.

S – Steward all God gives us to manage.

Biblical stewardship means to acknowledge that God is Owner of everything and that we have been entrusted with His possessions to use in His way for His purposes. We are tasked to look after His creation, using it, enjoying it, and caring for it.
A steward realizes that God is the provider of all we need to do His will. When we realize that we are not owners but managers of the resources we have been trusted with, this changes the choices we make as we employ these resources.

Stewardship is like a three-legged stool. The first leg is God's ownership of all. "Yours, O LORD, is the greatness and the power and the glory and the victory and the majesty, for all that is in the heavens and in the earth is yours . . ." (1 Chronicles 29:11).

The second leg is that God owns me. I have been redeemed (bought back) and now I belong to Jesus. ". . . You are not your own,

for you were bought with a price. So glorify God in your body" (1 Corinthians 6:19-20).
The third leg is that He gives me a portion of His resources to manage for His purposes in His way. "Calling ten of his servants, he gave them ten minas, and said to them, 'Engage in business until I come'" (Luke 19:13).

C – the Characteristics of a disciple

A wise mentor gave me a lesson on leadership. "What the people you lead need the most is your holiness."
What a challenge! "As obedient children, do not be conformed to the passions of your former ignorance, but as he who called you is holy, you also be holy in all your conduct, since it is written, 'You shall be holy, for I am holy'" (1 Peter 1:14-16).

Holiness means abiding in the one who is holy and allowing the life of Christ to flow through us. Holiness results only from a right relationship with God. Then the Holy Spirit will bring the qualities of life in Christ – the fruit described in Part 2 of this book.
Living a holy life makes a deep impression. Lighthouses do not generally sound horns; they just shine. C.S. Lewis wrote, in his booklet, Letters to an American Lady, "How little people know who think that holiness is dull. When one meets the real thing, it is irresistible. "60

Three exercises help us maintain holiness. First, we need to regularly evaluate our lives to see if we are still on course; mission drift is common in our lives as well as in organizations. Paul says, "Examine yourselves to see whether you are in the faith. Test yourselves" (2 Corinthians 13:5).
Second, we control our life. Self-control is the last aspect of the fruit the Holy Spirit reproduces in our lives. Without self- control, there is no discipleship.
The third exercise is daily surrendering our will to the Lord's will, "The martyred missionary to Ecuador. Jim Elliott wrote in his journal, "He is no fool who gives away what he cannot keep, to gain what he cannot lose." [2]

I – Invest in God's work.

The next stage in growing as a financial disciple is to invest in God's kingdom, learning to be radically generous in every aspect of our lives, to be a pipeline of God's grace and not an end station. Sadly, many pipelines are filled with holes or obstructions. A lot of what God puts into our finances never flows through the other end. How can it when debt and selfishness keep our spending circles open? We don't need
bigger pipes, just pipes that are kept in good repair. We glorify the Lord by being a clean, unblocked channel of Hs blessings. We don't need to hold back: God wants to give us more than we could ever hold!

God gives to us so we can keep on giving. He is the ultimate Generous Giver. It has been said that you are never more like Jesus than when you are giving. To love is to give.
God has given us countless blessings: a beautiful world in which to live, good things to enjoy, and most of all, salvation in Jesus that cost His life.
He gives so we can invest in His work. After receiving all the gifts for the building of the Temple, David realized that the people gave because God had given to them to give. *"But who am I, and who are my people, that we could give anything to you? Everything we have has come from you, and we give you only what you first gave us!"* (1 Chronicles 29:14, NLT).

P – Pray for people God is bringing to you to love, serve, and help develop.

In His prayer for the disciples, Jesus said to the Father, *"I have manifested your name to the people whom you gave me out of the world . . ."* (John 17:6).
I have set up discipleship ministries in over 25 nations and have never gone out to look for people to get these ministries started. God always gave them to me. He gave me people *"out of the world."* Although Jesus taught many, He discipled some and had a

special place for a few to whom He showed the secrets of the kingdom.

If we keep our eyes open, we can recognize people whom God is giving us to help. We will have a "connect" with them, a rapport, an almost-easy relationship.

L – Live out your faith day by day.

"Take My Life" is a beautiful hymn by Frances Havergal. [61]

> Take my life and let it be consecrated, Lord, to Thee.
> Take my moments and my days, let them flow in ceaseless praise.
> Take my hands and let them move at the impulse of Thy love.
> Take my feet and let them be swift and beautiful for Thee.
> Take my voice and let me sing always, only for my King.
> Take my lips and let them be filled with messages from Thee.
> Take my silver and my gold, not a mite would I withhold.
> Take my moments and my days, let them flow in ceaseless praise.

The financial disciple is surrounded by temptations. Jesus said, *"You cannot serve both God and money!"* We make daily choices – even moment-by-moment choices – in response to the many temptations of our consumer society.

If you have not already settled the question, How much is enough? the matter will continue to plague you. Can you learn to be content with what you have? Can you say, "This is enough," and set a limit on spending?

The financial disciple keeps himself free to respond to God's instructions. Are you free from debt that limits your freedom and restricts your availability for God's purposes?

E – Equip others to become financial disciples.

This entails biblical teaching on discovering God's will for a disciple in the area of finances and possessions. It is important, because Jesus said, *"Where your treasure is, there your heart will be also"* (Matthew 6:21).

Compass - finances God's way provides many tools to help equip others. *Building Your Finances God's Way* is one example. Many others have been especially designed for couples, businesspeople, students, or children.

Equipping is best done together, one on one with individuals or by taking people through a small group experience.

DAY 25: QUESTIONS TO PONDER

239

How have you seen money problems impacting those in your church?

Why do you think there is such a strong reluctance to discuss personal finances in our world today?

How do you talk to people about money?

DAY 25: QUESTIONS TO PONDER

DAY 26: FINANCIAL DISCIPLESHIP IN ACTION

KEY VERSE

"I tell you the truth, there is no one who has left home or brothers or sisters or mother or father or children or fields for my sake and for the sake of the gospel who will not receive in this age a hundred times as much—homes, brothers, sisters, mothers, children, fields, all with persecutions—and in the age to come, eternal life."

Mark 10:29-30

L et's look at a pair of financial disciples back in Paul's time. They endured many trials, sacrificed much, and worked hard at their trade. Learning from Paul how to be disciples in the midst of tough economic challenges both in Corinth and Ephesus, they discipled another leader, Apollos.

Priscilla and Aquila, friends of Paul and mentors to Apollos, demonstrate what can happen when a dedicated couple work together to build others up in the faith. Their story begins in a time of great prosperity in Rome. Aquila, a Jew from the Black Sea region of Pontus, and his wife, Priscilla, a Roman lady from an aristocratic family, together came into conflict with the decrees of Claudius, the Emperor.

Aquila had become a believer in Christ when the gospel reached Rome. Priscilla was from a nobler family than her husband's. Although they came from very different backgrounds, they loved each other with a love that was second only to their love for their newfound savior, Jesus Christ.

The emperor deemed himself not only the source of wisdom and leadership but also the only one to be worshipped as a god.

Aquila and Priscilla were steady in their faith, refusing to bow to Roman gods or worship Caesar. It cost them dearly.

They had to leave behind their home, their possessions, their thriving business, and move to Corinth in Greece. Convinced of the need to follow Christ unconditionally, they were prepared to suffer for Him. Are you?

AND THEY LEFT ALL AND FOLLOWED HIM.

"He is no fool who gives what he cannot keep to gain what he cannot lose." This saying from Jim Elliot, martyred missionary to the Auca Indians of Ecuador, makes us realize that life with Christ leads us to see differently what we must leave to fully follow Him and gain something far better. [62]

Aquila and Priscilla realized this and paid the price. They left all – their family, friends, and business – to move to Corinth. They heeded the piercing words of Jesus, *"If anyone would come after me, let him deny himself and take up his cross and follow me. For whoever would save his life will lose it, but*

whoever loses his life for my sake will find it. For what will it profit a man if he gains the whole world and forfeits his soul? Or what shall a man give in return for his soul?" (Matthew 16:24-26).

They also realized, on the other hand, the tremendous promise Jesus gave His followers, "Truly, I say to you, there is no one who has left house or brothers or sisters or mother or father or children or lands, for my sake and for the gospel, who will not receive a hundredfold now in this time, houses and brothers and sisters and mothers and children and lands, with persecutions, and in the age to come eternal life" (Mark 10:29-30).

Would you be prepared to leave your family, friends, and business if the Lord called you for His work?

WORKING AND LEARNING IN CORINTH

Paul, Aquila, and Priscilla settled down to earn money for their daily needs. These tentmakers of Corinth, who were also sail makers, would likely have had as much work as they could manage.

Aquila and Priscilla were observing Paul's work ethic day in and day out, seeing his commitment to not be a burden to anyone while preaching the gospel of Christ.
The three of them visited the Corinthian synagogue on the Sabbath, as was Paul's habit. They heard Paul expound the truths of the Old Testament, revealing Christ from the Scriptures. Later in his letter to the Corinthians, Paul wrote,
"For I resolved to know nothing while I was with you except Jesus Christ and him crucified" (1 Corinthians 2:2).
Aquilla and Priscilla learned from Paul his singlemindedness in following Christ not only in the Synagogue but also daily in their tent-making business.
The three stayed together for a little over a year and a half in Corinth, teaching the word of God among the believers in the city and witnessing daily in the marketplace to all who would listen.

During their time together, Aquila and Priscilla learned a great deal from Paul. They saw Paul wrestle with many thorny problems this new church in Corinth experienced. As disciples, they learned how to live in a large, corrupt city full of temptations – sex, idolatry, pagan power. No wonder Paul wrote later to the Corinthians, "No temptation has overtaken you that is not common to man. God is faithful, and he will not let you be tempted beyond your ability, but with the temptation he will also provide the way of escape, that you may be able to endure it" (1 Corinthians 10:13). Aquila and Priscilla learned this from their close contact with Paul in the rough, everyday life of Corinth.

Paul also described how they lived and worked in Corinth. "You, however, know all about my teaching, my way of life, my purpose, faith, patience, love, endurance," (2 Timothy 3:10, NIV). Aquila and Priscilla were constantly close to Paul and could observe all he did. This is the Oriental method of teaching, a method by example that has stood the test of time to this day. Indeed, Paul could say, "Follow my example, as I follow the example of Christ" (1 Corinthians 11:1, NIV).
They worked closely together to produce quality work. Aquila was

not green behind the ears, yet he placed himself under the experienced eye of Paul, eager to learn at the feet of the master.

As we will see later, when Aquila and Priscilla were alone in Ephesus, they got hold of Apollo and taught him what they had learned from Paul. To be really effective for Christ, each of us needs a mentor.
Do you have a "Paul" in your life? Someone who can disciple you and teach you how to disciple others?

IN EPHESUS

After Paul left them in Ephesus, the couple continued to work hard at building their business and developing their contacts. They were on their own in a strange city with the echo of Paul's words in their ears, "See you after the summer!"
Finding a suitable place around the Agora, the marketplace, was not difficult and they set up shop in this strategic location.

People would stop by to see their tents and other coverings and to talk about the state of the world with newcomers from far off places. Aquila and Priscilla would show their products of leather and cilicium, which is a cloth woven from the hair of the long-haired black goats of the middle east. Paul had made the same kind of black tents back in Tarsus, and they were widely used by trade caravans, nomads, and armies all over the region. But in addition to doing business, Aquila and Priscilla capitalized on these opportunities to tell others about "The Way."

Here they did not start a Christian church in the same manner as in Corinth. Instead, they joined the synagogue. To their surprise they met a brilliant Jew from Alexandria in Egypt. Apollos spoke persuasively about Jesus of Nazareth, describing accurately the facts around his life, death, and resurrection. But Apollos talked about Jesus as if he were a
figure of history rather than someone still at work in the world and in the hearts of men. The only baptism Apollos had heard of was

that of John, which was a baptism of repentance and expectancy of the imminent kingdom of God.

Aquila and Priscilla had observed how Paul took people apart to teach them privately. They had seen him teaching Timothy, Silas, and others. Paul had told them how he himself had been taught by Barnabas throughout the early years. They invited Apollos back to their home and started to teach him more accurately about Jesus. Priscilla and Aquila communicated to Apollos what it meant to have an intimate relationship with the risen Lord and Savior. They filled in the gaps of his knowledge until he learned the secret of the risen Lord at work in believers through the Holy Spirit.

After being baptized in the name of the Lord Jesus and receiving the Holy Spirit, Apollos's great gift of teaching became even more persuasive and urgent. Having come to the full knowledge of the truth and having received the power of the Holy Spirit, he felt the need to go to Greece. Aquila and Priscilla realized how valuable such a man would be in the newly established church at Corinth. Together with their small group of believers, they gave him a warm letter of introduction and sent him off with their prayers. Later, they received news back from Corinth about how Apollos had given help to those, who through God's grace, had become believers. "For with his strong arguments he defeated the Jews in public debates, proving from the Scriptures that Jesus is the Messiah" (Acts 18:28, GNT).

When Paul returned to Ephesus, he suffered harsh conditions along with the other believers. Their spiritual life was intense, but their physical existence was much more difficult. We see this in the words written to the Corinthians from Ephesus: *To the present hour we hunger and thirst, we are poorly dressed and buffeted and homeless, and we labor, working with our own hands. When reviled, we bless; when persecuted, we endure"* (1 Corinthians 4:11-12). And later, when saying farewell to the elders of Ephesus, he proved how deep an impression the hardship of his life there had made on him: *"You yourselves know that these hands ministered to my necessities and to those who were with me"* (Acts 20:34). While in Ephesus, Paul took no money or possessions from believers, saying, *"I coveted no one's silver or gold or apparel"* (Acts 20:33).

Aquila and Priscilla observed Paul's determination to work extremely hard for a living, not wanting to be a burden to anyone.

In the early spring of 53 A.D., abusive Jews made Paul's teaching in the synagogue impossible. Relocating to a portico in the city's gymnasium, he taught there each day from eleven until four while much of Ephesus would shut down in the heat of the day. Aquila and Priscilla brought their friends to the sessions in Tyrannus's gymnasium when their business was closed for lunch. For two years Paul held classes there, as did many other teachers, except that Paul's were without charge. Aquila and Priscilla played an important part in the funding of Paul's ministry.
Do you have an "Apollos?" Who is the Lord giving you to disciple and help further in their walk with the Lord?

MONEY OR CHRIST?

A Jewish high priest named Sceva had seven sons running a business as traveling exorcists. After witnessing Paul's miracles in the name of Jesus, they decided to add Jesus' name to their catalogue. Nothing remarkable happened until they reached the house of a demon-possessed man. They cried, "We command you in the name of Jesus, who Paul preaches
. . ." But before they could go any further, a strange voice came out of the man, saying *"Jesus I know, and Paul I know about, but who are you?"* (Acts 19:15, NIV). The possessed man jumped on them and beat them up, chasing them out of the house, "naked and bleeding."

This incident shook Ephesus. ". . . the Jews and Greeks living in Ephesus . . . were all seized with fear, and the name of the Lord *Jesus was held in high honor."* The effect on the young church was also very clear. Many believers confessed that they had dabbled in the occult and said they wanted to stop their habits of darkness. *"A*

*number who had practiced sorcery brought their scrolls together
and burned them publicly"* (Acts 19:19). As rolls of magical spells
and rare cabalistic writings went up in smoke, including some for
which magicians would have paid high prices, public opinion
reckoned that the value totaled the very considerable sum of fifty
thousand silver drachmas. This would have been equivalent to the
total salaries of 150 men working for a whole year! These people
did not wring their hands over the cost; they decisively repented
and turned from their sins.

The citizens of Ephesus were confronted with a watershed choice:
make money in a way that displeases God – or follow Christ. You
can read the story in Acts 19:11-20.
How about you? Is there anything in your life that needs to stop in
obedience to the Lord? Even if it costs a lot of money?

MORE MONEY TROUBLES

The Jews had secured imperial protection from Augustus for
money raised to support the Temple in Jerusalem: anyone
interfering with the collection was liable to the same penalty as
those interfering with pagan temples. Ephesus was the center for
collecting the temple tax for the whole area.
Temple treasurers, nervous about the drop in funds due to the
conversion of hundreds of Jews to the Christian way, decided to
take action.
Paul had not told the converts to stop paying, but the decline was
significant as more and more contributed to Paul's requests to
help the Christian church in Jerusalem.

The treasurers lodged a formal complaint to the Proconsul of Asia,
Marcus Junius Silanus, alleging that Paul was misappropriating
money meant for the Temple. Silanus was a
cousin of the reigning emperor Claudius and his adopted son,
Nero. As a man of stature and justice, he chose to hear the case
himself. He ordered Paul's arrest in the autumn of 53 A. D.
As a Roman citizen, Paul was imprisoned in the room of the
Praetorian Guard at the proconsular palace. If found guilty, he

would be fed to the hungry animals at the next gladiatorial games in Ephesus. Of course, his friends Aquila and Priscilla, Timothy, and others came to see him frequently. He was allowed to go about the city chained to a Roman soldier, and he continued teaching at the school of Tyrannus.

Paul had lots of time to pray. The soldiers heard him pray with Aquila and Priscilla, who were never afraid to associate themselves with Paul, even in the company of the Praetorian Guard. They saw the power of the gospel even in those circumstances. *"Now I want you to know, brothers and sisters, that what has happened to me has actually served to advance* the gospel. As a result, it has become clear throughout the whole palace guard and to everyone else that I am in chains for Christ. And because of my chains, most of the brothers and sisters have become confident in the Lord and dare all the more to proclaim the gospel without fear" (Philippians 1:12-14).

Aquila and Priscilla and others who were with Paul in his confinement became bold to speak about Christ in these unsettled days in Ephesus.

Followers of Jesus will most likely have to travel the road He traveled: trials, misunderstandings, and persecutions. Can you detect God's purpose in having you travel this road?

BUSINESS OR BELIEF?

Ephesus hosted a great festival every spring. Those devoted to the Mother Goddess came to the festival of Artemisia, where trade, worship, and gaiety made it the highlight of the year. Crowds thronged the streets. This was an opportunity for ministry that the tentmakers did not want to miss.

It was the prime selling time for the important guild of silversmiths. Their replicas of the Artemis statue and small silver temples were normally in heavy demand. This year, 55 A.D. was different. The silversmiths suffered a considerable slump. Why? Because of the successful mission led by Paul and Aquila and Priscilla, hundreds of visitors uncharacteristically refused to buy the products. Many had become Christians and were treating the festival of Artemisia as a holiday outing, a chance to hear Paul again and to meet fellow believers. Others, new converts during the festival itself, suddenly had no more desire to engage in idol worship. The silversmiths, having lost a lot of business, were very uncomfortable.

One of the biggest employers and chairman of the guild, Demetrius was in a terrible rage about the loss of business and his resulting loss of power in the city. A huge riot ensued.

The Chief Executive Officer of the city was a sensible man who managed to quiet the crowd and restore some semblance of order. He made them thoroughly ashamed of themselves and declared the assembly closed.

After this, Paul called all the disciples together and spoke an encouraging word to them. He then left to go to Greece, to Philippi.

It was very probable that Demetrius and his fellows at the silversmith's guild would not leave it there. They would have done all they could to make life sour for the believers who remained in Ephesus – especially businesspeople like Aquila and Priscilla, who were foreign to the city.

They probably received a lot of resistance from the local business community.

Sometimes financial disciples must be prepared to minister in very challenging situations, making moral and ethical decisions that cost money. Are you evaluating your decisions in work and business? Are they conforming to God's standards of goodness?

BACK IN ROME

Early the next year, 57 A.D., Aquila and Priscilla were back in Rome. They knew that their friend Paul longed to go to Rome, and it is plausible to think that Paul might have asked them to go there to prepare a tent-making business.

Paul finally arrived to be with them in March of 60 A.D. Once more they were together, this time in Rome, the capital of the world.

We do not know how long Aquila and Priscilla stayed in Rome. Paul was arrested, acquitted, and arrested again for the last time

in the summer of 66 A.D. Where Paul went after his release is uncertain. He may have gone to Spain, as he had previously desired. Clement of Rome wrote thirty years later to the Corinthians that Paul reached "the farthest bounds of the west." After the fire in Rome in the year 64 A.D., the persecution of Christians was particularly vicious. The crazy dictator Nero was terrifying in his relentless pursuit of believers, whom he blamed for the destruction of Rome – but which he himself had instigated. It seems that Aquila and Priscilla went back with Timothy to Ephesus.
Paul wrote to the Christians in Rome, "Greet Prisca and Aquila, my fellow workers in Christ Jesus, who risked their necks for my life, to whom not only I give thanks but all the churches of the Gentiles give thanks as well. Greet also the church in their house" (Romans 16:3-5).

The essence of discipleship is reflected in the way Aquila and Priscilla first gave themselves to Paul, then to Apollos, and then other believers from various churches they helped plant.
"They even did more than we had hoped, for their first action was to give themselves to the Lord and to us, just as God wanted them to do" (2 Corinthians 8:5, NLT).

Exercising our gifts for the benefit of helping others grow spiritually will merit eternal reward. The extent to which we can invest in people's lives varies according to our gifts and opportunities. Paul wrote that some sow, others water, and others reap; and yet each receive their due awards.
"I planted, Apollos watered, but God gave the growth. So neither he who plants nor he who waters is anything, but only God who gives the growth. He who plants and he who waters are one, and each will receive his wages according to his labor" (1 Corinthians 3:6-8).

DAY 26: QUESTIONS TO PONDER

251

It is said of Aquila and Priscilla that they were faithful to the end. What is needed for someone to say the same about you?

Have you ever had a situation in which a decision to obey Christ has cost you money?

Can you give yourself to a "Paul" as a mentor for you and to accompany an "Apollos" along the path of financial discipleship?

Aquila and Priscilla ministered as a couple. How could you use your marriage and your home more effectively to serve the Lord?

DAY 27: FISHERS OF MEN

KEY VERSE

"And he said to them, 'Follow me, and I will make you fishers of men.'"

Matthew 4:19

W hile walking by the Sea of Galilee, he saw two brothers, Simon (who is called Peter) and Andrew his brother, casting a net into the sea, for they were fishermen. And he said to them,
'Follow me, and I will make you fishers of men.' Immediately they left their nets and followed him. And going on from there he saw two other brothers, James the son of Zebedee and John his brother, in the boat with Zebedee their father, mending their nets, and he called them. Immediately they left the boat and their father and followed him" (Matthew 4:18-22).

What was Jesus mean by inviting Simon and Andrew to become fishers of men? The analogy seemed to fit well with these men who had been fishermen all their lives, in a family business. They lived in a fishing village near the sea of Galilee. Using the words 'fishing' and 'catching' would be familiar to them. However, fishing for men would sound very odd.
Jesus used their everyday language to illustrate their new assignment; not any theological construct. Becoming a fisher of men is not something assigned only to those in the Zebedee & Sons family business. Jesus gives the same the sacred assignment to each of us.

He would not have asked them theological questions, because they would not have understood. They were fishermen, not Jewish leaders or teachers of the law. Jesus used language that they would easily relate to.
These fishermen were men who fished every night to bring in their catch the next
Morning before going to the market to sell their haul. And then return to mend their nets for the next night. They were ordinary, hard-working guys who wanted to look after their families and enjoy their fishing. They had no sense of their own importance. They were uneducated people and not looking to any high calling or seeing a future vision, yet Jesus called them to participate in a world-changing endeavor - just as He calls you and I today.

To be a fisher of men in the 21st century means we must expand our horizons and look beyond the bubble we live in. These fishermen-turned-disciples most
likely had no idea they would ever leave Galilee. But they most certainly did. . Andrew travelled nations around the Black Sea. Thomas and Bartholomew went as far as India and James went all the way to Spain. Peter travelled to Rome. When called to become 'fishers of men' we are also called to leave our comfort zones and expand our horizon.
Our commission is exactly the same as it was for the original fishers of men in Galilee.
It brings great joy to hear that someone has accepted Christ, joy not only here but also in heaven. Jesus, an authority on heaven, says, *"Just so, I tell you, there is joy before the angels of God over one sinner who repents"* (Luke 15:10). To hear someone say, "Thank you for showing me the way," moves me to thankfulness for God's grace.

THE ARCHER

 Did you know that there are five expressions of the Great Commission in the New Testament?
Dave Wirgau of The Navigators pictured this in what he called "The Archer Illustration" to show how you can reach the nations

through making disciples in response to each of these five challenges. Dave took a piece of paper and began drawing.
First, he drew a target and told us to turn in the Bible to Mark 16:15. We read, "Go into all the world and proclaim the gospel to the whole creation." The emphasis on that illustration was the world. He drew the world as the target.

Next he drew a stick figure of an archer shooting an arrow toward the target. We opened our Bibles to John 20:21. Jesus said to His disciples, "As the Father has sent me, even so I am sending you." As the archer in this illustration, Jesus is the one sending the arrow toward the target, which is the world. We are the arrow.

Then he put a bow and a bow string into the hand of the archer and asked us to turn to Acts 1:8. In that Great
Commission verse, Jesus says, "You will receive power when the Holy Spirit has come upon you, and you will be my witnesses in Jerusalem and in all Judea and Samaria, and to the end of the earth." Dave began to explain how this passage describes the power source for the arrow to be launched. Jesus is the archer, and the bow of the Holy Spirit empowers us to be the arrow. Drawing as he spoke, he completed the arrow and then exaggerated the tip.

As he made the tip larger, he asked us to look at Luke 24:47. *". . . the Christ should suffer and on the third day rise from the dead, and that repentance for the forgiveness of sins should be proclaimed in his name to all nations, beginning from Jerusalem."* The emphasis of this commission verse is the content of the message: repentance and forgiveness of sin to be taken to the world. The content is the tip of the arrow, which should fly into human hearts.
Last, he asked us to turn to Matthew 28, verses 18 through 20. We read, ". . . All authority in heaven and on earth has been given to me. Go therefore and make disciples of all nations, baptizing them in the name of the Father and of the Son and of the Holy Spirit, teaching them to observe all that I have commanded you. And behold, I am with you always, to the end of the age."

The emphasis of Matthew 28 was making disciples. This is represented by the shaft of the arrow, the most effective means by which the tip – the message – can be delivered to the world.

It struck me that Dave was doing that with me. He was investing in me, passing on to me the truth of this great commission. He was actually discipling me as we talked about this command to *"go and make disciples of all nations."*

This illustration of the archer shooting an arrow toward the target helped me understand the Great Commission: Jesus (the archer) uses the power of the Holy Spirit (the bow) to send us (the two-part arrow, tip and shaft). The tip of our arrow is the message of repentance and forgiveness of sin. The shaft connects the tip at one end of the arrow to the bow string
at the other end; this is the process of disciple making in the whole world (the target). When you make disciples, you are part of fulfilling the Great Commission Jesus gave us.
What a privilege to share in the harvest of the work of the Holy Spirit among the nations!

THE HARVEST

 The concept of sowing and reaping is a foundational expression of working in the kingdom of God. There can be no reaping of a harvest without sowing. It is how the kingdom expands.
Paul uses the process of sowing and reaping in a financial context in 2 Corinthians 9:6,7. "The point is this: whoever sows sparingly will also reap sparingly, and whoever sows bountifully will also reap bountifully. Each one must give as he has decided in his heart, not reluctantly or under compulsion, for God loves a cheerful giver."

We discussed the concept of financial sowing and reaping on Day 22. But in this parable of the sower, which you can read
in Mark 4:1-20, Jesus pictures sowing and reaping in terms of people. A sower went out into his field to sow seeds, fully

expecting his work to yield a good harvest. Jesus explained that the seed was the word of God, and the field was a human heart. Some seed fell on a path, where birds came and ate it all. Jesus explained that the birds in this allegory represent the devil, who takes away the word from those whose hearts are hardened to it. Part of the seed was sown in shallow, stony soil. It sprouted quickly but withered when the sun came out, because the soil was not deep enough to support strong roots. The sun represents the heat of problems that burned out the weak- rooted, undernourished plants; they couldn't survive the tough times.

Another part of the seed was sown in soil full of weeds and thorns. The young shoots were crowded out, unable to get the light, water, and nutrients they needed to grow. Jesus likened these young shoots to people who make a start but get tempted by *the cares of the world and the deceitfulness of riches and the desires for other things"* (Mark 4:19), focusing on those instead of the word. But some seeds were sown in good, rich soil, growing into healthy plants that bore lots of fruit – thirty, sixty, or even a hundred times as much as the starting seed.
Making financial disciples is sowing the word of God into people's lives. Like the farmer, we are not responsible for the yield: that is God's job. We can, however, contribute to the growth.

We can pray for people we are discipling, that they will be protected from the evil one.
We can help soften the hard ground of people's hearts by befriending them, spending time with them, loving and serving them. We can water parched fields by being a pipeline of God's blessings to their lives. It has been said that people will only accept the message if they can accept the messenger.
We can help take away the stones and rocks of objection to the word. These are often the result of past experiences people have had – sometimes at the hands of professing Christians – that gave them a wrong impression of God and hardened them to His message. Sometimes there are intellectual or conceptual questions that we could counter through respectful reasoning,

especially when it feels more like care and mutual exploration than winning a debate.

We can help take away the weeds of materialism and the deceitful power of money by sharing our personal experience of finding our ladder leaning against the wrong wall. Who wants to spend a lifetime pursuing a dream that ends up being hollow, or even worse, a nightmare? Perhaps our experience of understanding and applying God's word could help them learn how to overcome anxiety and worry about never having enough.

Given the obstacles, some won't grow to maturity. But the exhilarating news is that some will! God will see to it that some respond to His word, allowing it to take root and grow and yield an outsized harvest.
Recall in our earlier discussion of the fruit of the Spirit (in Part 2 of this book) that we briefly described the three parts of most fruit.

First, there is a stem that connects the fruit to the nourishing parent tree. This reflects being connected to Christ from whom we receive all needed spiritual nourishment to grow.
The second part of the fruit – the body itself – is meant to be consumed, supporting life in ourselves and others. This represents the fruit of the Spirit.
The third part of fruit is its seeds, each of which has the potential to grow into a new plant and bear more fruit. Each individual you help to grow in Christ has the potential to help others grow. This is the essence of making disciples: from one apple seed, many apples can grow! "The Power of One" will be further illustrated on Day 29.

SHINING LIKE STARS

 Some years ago I attended a global conference on discipling business and professional people in Atlanta, Georgia. The conference theme was "Shining Like Stars," taken from Daniel 12:3. *"And those who are wise shall shine like the brightness of the sky*

above; and those who turn many to righteousness, like the stars forever and ever."
In the construction of this verse, *"Those who are wise"* stand parallel to *"those who turn many to righteousness,"* which suggests that wise people are those who lead many into a right relationship with God and help them learn to live it out.
This suggests two groups: those who are wise (literally, "the teachers," those who teach others), and those who are leaders, sharing their faith and influencing many to turn to righteousness. God will honor their faithfulness. They shall shine out like the brightness of the universe and like the stars forever and ever.

Proverbs 11:30 tells us that *"The fruit of the righteous is a tree of life, and whoever captures souls is wise."* A person who wins souls is wise, and Daniel assures us that the wise shall shine as brightly as the sun's brilliance. Those who turn sinners to righteousness will glitter like stars forever.
James, the brother of Jesus, caught His vision. He encouraged believers to go after those who stray from the faith, to refuse to let them go. *"My brothers, if anyone among you wanders from the truth and someone brings him back, let him know*
that whoever brings back a sinner from his wandering will save his soul from death and will cover a multitude of sins" (James 5:19-20).

We are to do our absolute utmost to introduce those outside of the kingdom to the love of Christ. We are the ones to whom He entrusted this task. There is a significant opportunity for you to make an immediate impact in this day and age, just as there was back then. Jesus said, "The harvest is plentiful but the workers are few" (Matthew 9:37, NIV).

THE CALLING OF THE TWELVE

An often-told joke goes … Two women were walking down a street in New York City when they spotted a frog. The frog looked up and said, "I used to be a handsome, wealthy stockbroker, but I was turned into a frog. If one of you kisses me, I will be turned back into my original self. And I will be mighty grateful."

One of the women stooped down, picked up the frog and placed him in her purse. The two friends walked on for a while, but the other finally got curious and asked, "Aren't you going to kiss the frog and turn him back to what he was?"
"Uh, uh," she replied. "I'd rather have a talking frog."

Of course, the lady is supposed to kiss the frog, starting a transformation process in which the young prince (or stockbroker) is set free to reach his full potential. That's
how the story should go, but the clever joke is that a talking frog might be more entertaining – and less hassle – than a handsome, wealthy stockbroker who could turn out to be
a narcissist.

Funny joke, but let's go deeper. If we think of the woman as a believer with the opportunity to disciple someone (the frog in need of transformation), she completely dismisses the frog's needs and her supernatural opportunity in favor of the status quo – keeping the poor frog as a freak novelty. I wonder how she will feel looking into the eyes of Jesus at the bema seat when the episode is replayed.
Neither she nor the frog reached their full potential. How many of us accept the status quo rather than work to develop our gifts and opportunities to be workers in the waiting harvest?

Jesus selected His followers very carefully. In fact, He spent an entire night in prayer before choosing them.
"In these days he went out to the mountain to pray, and all night he continued in prayer to God. And when day came, he called his disciples and chose from them twelve, whom he named apostles: Simon, whom he named Peter, and Andrew his brother, and James and John, and Philip, and Bartholomew,
and Matthew, and Thomas, and James the son of Alphaeus, and Simon who was called the Zealot, and Judas the son of James, and Judas Iscariot, who later became a traitor" (Luke 6:12-16).
After choosing His disciples, Jesus invested His life into them for the next three and a half years, while living and traveling together,

teaching them and training them to continue the work after He left them.

The disciples had to learn to surrender their hearts and minds to God and be willing to be discipled by Jesus. We also need people who will help us to understand the Bible and apply its truths to our lives. Just like the twelve disciples, we too will struggle with life's challenges, and we need encouragement and help from experienced disciples to stay on track and persevere.
Note the words Jesus used when He called the disciples in Matthew 4:19. He didn't say, "Follow me and you will become fishers of men." Instead, He said, *"Follow me, and I will make you fishers of men."* The inference is that Jesus does most of the heavy lifting once we make ourselves available and follow Him. He transforms us into disciple makers when we surrender and invite the Holy Spirit to live His life through us.

DAY 27: QUESTIONS TO PONDER

262

What does it look like to be a "fisher of men" in our world today?

What are you doing to help fulfill the Great Commission?

How can you recognize people who are responding to the gospel?

DAY 28: HOW JESUS TRAINED THE TWELVE

KEY VERSE

"He appointed twelve (whom he also named apostles) so that they might be with him, and he might send them out to preach."

Mark 3:14

Well Done – Part 4: Making Financial Disciples

While traveling on a mission in the countries of southern and central Africa, I constantly heard an interesting comment from pastors I met. "Christianity in Africa is a mile wide and an inch deep!" I immediately realized that this was accurate not only in Africa but also in the church worldwide.
In Zimbabwe and Zambia I gazed at the thundering Victoria Falls on the Zambezi River. In Botswana I camped in the wide expanse of the beautiful Okavango delta with its impressive diversity of animal life. There is a great contrast between the two rivers. The Okavango swells in the hills of Angola, flowing south until it reaches a huge expanse of sand, a desert in Botswana. For a while, the river expands and allows life to flourish in an amazing riot of diversity as plants bloom and wildlife migrates to take advantage of the river's temporary expanse.

But then Angola's rain stops, the delta dries up, the Okavango River disappears, leaving dry salt pans as plants wither and wildlife retreats. This is an analogy of what happens when some people find Christ but fail to drink regularly at the springs of living water. They dry up and become barren.

In contrast, the Zambezi River, which has its source in northern Zambia, flows through six countries and is constantly fed by tributaries. It is the main supplier of fresh water and fish to the populations of these regions. The Zambezi runs through many game reserves and national parks, providing sustenance to a diverse array of fish, birds, and game. It powers two huge electricity-generating stations. Home to immense wet plains, the river basin is responsible for the climatic regulation of a rich ecosystem of savannahs and humid forests that surround it. It sustains life because it is constantly fed with water from a wide drainage area. This river is fruitful, year round.

Just like the Zambezi, we believers need to be constantly nourished, fed, and watered to become mature followers of Christ who can help others enjoy freedom and fullness in Christ.
I believe the best way to do this is to follow the methods of Jesus Himself, who trained twelve men whom "He appointed . . . so that they might be with him, and he might send them out
. . ." (Mark 3:14).

A classic book that explains Jesus' methods is The Master Plan of Evangelism by Robert Coleman. 63
He explains that Jesus' methods were actually Jesus Himself! His presence day by day with the disciples taught them all they needed to know, demonstrated to them all they needed to be, and showed that the way to fulfill His commission was to make other disciples to carry on the work. His method was life on life. Coleman explains eight key activities in the disciple-making process of Jesus. Let's briefly look at each of these.

1. SELECTION

 Jesus' concern was not with programs to reach multitudes but with men whom the multitudes would follow.

Christ did not call religious leaders or wealthy people to His service. He called ordinary working people. Who had hearts to leave what they were doing to follow Him, wherever He would lead them. They often found it difficult to grasp what Jesus was telling them, but they persisted despite failing time and again. The only exception was Judas who never really gave his heart and mind to Christ, being focused on gaining wealth instead of knowing Christ and following Him. He was a lover of money. He complained about Mary taking expensive ointment to anoint Jesus' feet. "He said this, not because he cared about the poor, but because he was a thief, and having charge of the moneybag he used to help himself to what was put into it" (John 12:6). He followed Christ for the wrong reasons. Later, he later sold Jesus for money, but he actually sold himself.
We read that Peter and John were "uneducated, common men, they were astonished. And they recognized that they had been with Jesus." (Acts 4:13)

They had been with Jesus and therefore completely changed into people who were able to share the truth about Him to a group of religious leaders. Previously slow to understand the truth about Jesus, these uneducated men were transformed in their understanding of the terms of salvation.

Jesus' call was a prayerful call. When Jesus raised Lazarus from the dead, we read that He prayed for a moment and used just a few words (see John 11:38-44).
But when choosing His disciples, He prayed all night! This underscores the importance of His mission, which was to be carried out by these twelve men.

His call was a commissioning call. An apostle is one who is sent out. It was used among the Athenians to designate the admiral of the fleet, who would be commissioned and sent out with authority.
His call was a personal call. He called them by name. I believe He looked them in the eye and said, "Come, Peter, (fill in your own name) follow me, and I will make you a fisher of men."
His call was a sacrificial call. They had to leave their places of work, follow Jesus, and trust in Him for provision.
Have you heard Jesus' call to you? Are you calling people whom God brings across your path to follow Jesus and become fishers of men themselves?

2. ASSOCIATION

 Jesus said, "Come to me, all who labor and are heavy laden, and I will give you rest. Take my yoke upon you, and learn from me, for I am gentle and lowly in heart, and you will find rest for your souls. For my yoke is easy, and my burden is light" (Matthew 11:28-30). The Lord invites us to work with him in a "yoke," sharing equally the burden of our work. We will then
learn to follow Jesus as He leads, experiencing Him working in close proximity.
The principle of association is proximity to Jesus, being with Him. He gave us the illustration of the vine and the branches. "I am the vine; you are the branches. Whoever abides in me and I in him, he it is that bears much fruit, for apart from me you can do nothing" (John 15:5).
Someone got very good Irish advice at a renowned horse race when he asked, "Whatever is that old nag doing in this race?" The answer was, "I know he has no chance of winning, but the association will do him good." Abiding in the vine assures us of association with the best possible life partner – the Lord Jesus Christ. Then the dynamic life of the vine can flow through us and bear fruit.
Are you spending time with the Lord each day in close fellowship? Disciple making involves spending quality time with those you are helping.

3. CONSECRATION

Consecration means to separate yourself from anything that would keep you from your growing in your relationship with a perfect God. It carries the meaning of sanctification, holiness, or purity.

The standard is high. "As obedient children, do not be conformed to the passions of your former ignorance, but as he who called you is holy, you also be holy in all your conduct, since it is written, "You shall be holy, for I am holy" (1 Peter 1:14-16).

We can see an illustration of consecration when Joshua gave the Israelites a command and a promise before entering the promised Land after wandering for so many years in the wilderness: *"Then Joshua said to the people, 'Consecrate yourselves, for tomorrow the LORD will do wonders among you'"* (Joshua 3:5).

Being consecrated is crucial to our relationship with God. We are not to be conformed to the standards of the world but renewed to know what God is asking us to do. "I appeal to you therefore, brothers, by the mercies of God, to present your bodies as a living sacrifice, holy and acceptable to God, which is your spiritual worship. Do not be conformed to this world, but be transformed by the renewal of your mind, that by testing you may discern what is the will of God, what is good and acceptable and perfect" (Romans 12:1-2).

Have you dedicated your life totally to the Lord, to be set apart for His work through you? The dedication of the people you are discipling will be largely determined by your example. You cannot lead anyone further than you have gone yourself!

4. IMPARTATION

Jesus realized that the disciples were not able to live up to God's standards. You cannot lift yourself up by your own shoelaces. It is impossible. You need a force outside of yourself to empower what Jesus is asking of you.

Jesus will empower us, just as He did for the disciples when He said, "Receive the Holy Spirit" (John 20:22). In receiving His Spirit, He was to impart God's love for a fallen world.
Jesus prayed to the Father, "As You sent me . . . I have sent them" (John 17:18). Robert Coleman wrote, "Jesus was God in revelation; but the Spirit was God in operation."

The Holy Spirit works to carry out the eternal plan of salvation – through disciples like you and I. He prepared the way for their ministry, helping disciples to know what to say; "… do not be anxious beforehand what you are to say, but say whatever is given you in that hour, for it is not you who speak, but the Holy Spirit. (Mark 13:11).
It is also the task of the Holy Spirit to "convict the world concerning sin and righteousness and judgment." (John 16:8). The Holy Spirit also guides people to come to know the full truth about God. (John 16:13).

Discipleship will always be the work of the Spirit. Consequently, your primary responsibility in discipling others is to yield control of your life to the Holy Spirit. As you share your life with someone close to you, pray that they realize how great the power is that works within them. "For this reason I bow my knees before the Father, from whom every family in heaven and on earth is named, that according to the riches
of his glory he may grant you to be strengthened with power through his Spirit in your inner being" (Ephesians 3:14-16).

5. DEMONSTRATION

 Jesus said to His disciples, "I have given you an example, that you also should do just as I have done to you" (John 13:15).
While watching people give their offerings in the temple, Jesus taught the disciples about giving.
He demonstrated how to converse with the Father in prayer and taught them to do the same.

Jesus demonstrated the importance of the Holy Scriptures and how to use them, taking time to impress on His followers the meaning of Bible passages. He was constantly quoting the Scriptures in His conversation with them.

Jesus was a living lesson!   Robert Coleman wrote, "People are looking for a demonstration, not an explanation. We are the exhibit!"

It is said that people don't care how much we know until they have seen how much we care. The disciples saw this very clearly as Jesus poured Himself out for the needy.

Those of us wishing to disciple others, must be prepared to be vulnerable. We must let people into our lives, not maintaining a mask of self-sufficiency but allowing people to see how we are being dependent on God in times of trouble. Jesus gave the disciples a glimpse of his human nature when He cried at Lazarus's death, wept over Jerusalem's future, and suffered almost unbearable stress in Gethsemane at his impending trials.

Can you understand what the Lord is doing in your life as you deal with its struggles and challenges? Be vulnerable, letting people see the realities of your life and learn how your relationship with Jesus is shaping and molding you. This lesson is worth far more than study or lectures.

6. DELEGATION

 After a full day of teaching crowds of people, Jesus delivered another powerful living lesson. "As evening approached, the disciples came to him and said, "This is a remote place, and it's already getting late. Send the crowds away, so they can go to the villages and buy themselves some food."

Jesus replied, "They do not need to go away. You give them something to eat" (Matthew 14:15-16).

Jesus did not do the multiplying of the food by Himself. If so, there would have been a huge pile of food in front of Him.

Instead, He allowed the disciples to multiply the food as they went along, feeding at least five thousand men. His approach was, "You do it! I will work through you!"
When Jesus was beginning His third ministry tour through Galilee, He began to send the disciples out by themselves.

When going out on mission, they were told to travel light, without unnecessary burden. "Take nothing for your journey, no staff, nor bag, nor bread, nor money; and do not have two tunics.: (Luke 9:3) This forced their dependence on the Lord's provision. He sent them out two by two, emphasizing the need for fellowship and mutual encouragement.
He gave them "authority and power" (verse 1).

He reaffirmed the purpose of going: "to proclaim the kingdom of God and to heal" (verse 2).
He instructed them not to burden themselves with excess baggage and not to take money or food with them. This forced their dependence on the Lord's provision.
They were told to concentrate on people who would receive them, who were open to their message, with whom the disciples could follow up their work.
What tasks can you give those you are helping grow as financial disciples? They can learn a lot by carrying out tasks such as teaching others – perhaps co-leading a small group financial discipleship study.

7. SUPERVISION

 Jesus' asked the disciples to share their experiences with the group. They were to report back and evaluate what they had learned. "The seventy-two returned with joy, saying, "Lord, even the demons are subject to us in your name!" (Luke 10:17).
Jesus continually reviewed how the disciples were applying His teaching, so that he could lead, correct and encourage them.
When the disciples experienced something or heard something from Him that they didn't fully grasp, Jesus taught by example,

giving assignments and regular evaluations in order to bring out the best in His followers. The disciples' encounters with life situations enabled Jesus to pinpoint His teaching on specific needs, spelling out the truth in concrete terms of practical experience. His style of teaching by example, assignment, and constant checkup was calculated to bring out the best in His followers.

Jesus corrected the disciples' attitude toward others who were ministering in Jesus' name but who were not a part of the apostolic group. "'Master, we saw someone casting out demons in your name, and we tried to stop him, because he does not follow with us.' But Jesus said to him, 'Do not stop him, for the one who is not against you is for you'" (Luke 9:49-50).

When the disciples wanted the Lord to call down fire on some people for their unbelief, Jesus actually told them off for being hard hearted. "And when his disciples James and John saw it, they said, 'Lord, do you want us to tell fire to come down from heaven and consume them?' But he turned and rebuked them" (Luke 9:54-56).

Are you regularly evaluating your own walk with the Lord and helping others to do the same?

8. REPRODUCTION

Jesus used the analogy of a vine to explain the work of both the vine (Himself) and the branches (believers in Him) in order to bear fruit.

Jesus wanted His disciples to reproduce His likeness and His ministry in the lives of believers.

.In his prayer, Jesus said to the Father, "I glorified you on earth, having accomplished the work that you gave me to do" (John 17:4). What was this work? To disciple the people God gave Him. "I have manifested your name to the people whom you gave me out of the world. Yours they were, and you gave them to me, and they have kept your word" (John 17:6).

Then the Lord discussed the plan to further the kingdom. "As you sent me into the world, so I have sent them into the world. I do not ask for these only, but also for those who will believe in me through their word" (John 17:18, 20).

For Jesus' strategy to work, He placed a high degree of dependence on the faithfulness of His chosen disciples. He was not primarily concerned with how large a group may be, but on the faithfulness of the disciples to reproduce and teach others to reproduce in the same way.

Christ's Great Commission explained His strategy in His command to "make disciples of all nations" (Matthew 28:19). Making disciples means to "go," "baptize," and "teach."
The Great Commission is not only referring to go to the ends of the earth to preach the gospel (Mark 16:15), nor to baptize converts in the name of the Trinity, nor
to teach them Biblical principles, important as there are. The main focus of His commission is to "make disciples" – to help people grow to become like Jesus.

Who are you discipling right now? Can you ask the Lord to give you someone – or even a small group – to disciple?

DAY 28: QUESTIONS TO PONDER

What has been your experience in being discipled and discipling others?

How are you currently being discipled yourself?

How are you discipling others?

DAY 29: THE POWER OF ONE

KEY VERSE

"I have manifested your name to the people whom you gave me out of the world. Yours they were, and you gave them to me, and they have kept your word."

John 17:6

Twice I have been given the challenge of pioneering a European discipleship ministry. The first was with Christian Businessmen's Committees (CBMC) in 1989. Little did I know at that time that a couple of months later the Berlin Wall would collapse, opening the former communist nations of Eastern Europe to business and to the gospel!

The second opportunity came in 2007, when I was asked by Crown Financial Ministries to set up a movement to teach people biblical finances. Little did I know that just a few months later the world would plunge into a financial crisis!

It seemed like the Lord was preparing Europe to receive these ministries of evangelism and discipleship. In 1990, borders were changing and in 2008, economic conditions changed drastically. Paul wrote that God *"determined allotted periods and the boundaries of their dwelling place, that they should seek God, and perhaps feel their way toward him and find him"* (Acts 17:26-27). When God wants to start a movement, He not only gathers people to do the job but often also changes political and economic situations to help the new movement.

To begin the building of a multinational Christian movement, the Lord gave me a promise from Isaiah 60:22. "The least of you will become a thousand, the smallest a mighty nation. I am the Lord; in its time I will do this swiftly."

The Lord began to build these movements swiftly. As I am writing, the movement of Christian business and professional people is now active in over 30 nations in Europe. Many people have found Christ and been discipled – not by me, but by people whom I had recruited, mentored, and trained. The second movement, despite a severe setback in 2012, continues to grow. We are now teaching *finances – God's way* to people in over 20 nations in Europe.

As I look back on what has happened in the national movements I have helped to get going, I can testify to the power of the promise in Isaiah 60:22. Thousands are serving in these movements as we speak.

Where did I find the people to lead the ministry in all these nations? Well, I didn't. God did. My part was to ask God for F.A.T. people (Faithful, Available, and Teachable). My part was to look around and see who God was giving me and then meet them, pray for them, and accompany them in starting a discipleship ministry in their city and nation.

My guiding principle was taken from what Jesus prayed in John 17:6. "I have manifested your name to the people whom you gave me out of the world. Yours they were, and you gave them to me, and they have kept your word." God gave me people "out of the world."

Just as Jesus said, I did not need to pray for the world or whole nations – just a few people. "I am praying for them. I am not praying for the world but for those whom you have given me, for they are yours" (John 17:9).

I shared the word with them. Then I prayed for those God had given me that they too would do the same and reach others with the gospel, discipling them. *"I do not ask for these only, but also for those who will believe in me through their word"* (John 17:20).

WHO'S YOUR "ONE"?

Who do you think of first, when you consider neighbors, friends, family members or co-workers who do not yet know God? Be sure God fervently desires their salvation. "The Lord is not slow to fulfill his promise as some count slowness, but is patient toward you, not wishing that any should perish, but that all should reach repentance. (2 Peter 3:9) Remember, God is not asking for your ability but your availability.

I would like to challenge you to pray and ask God to lead you to one person that you can interact with, befriend, and start a conversation with.

Every person is of immeasurable value to God for three reasons. First, because that person was created by God in His image and is loved and wanted by Him. Second, because of what he or she cost – the precious blood of Jesus. Third, because of what he or she can become – a child of God
who can love God and neighbors and have a capacity for spiritual reproduction.

Your "one" is someone who has given their life to Christ but may still be early in their spiritual walk and who needs help to learn, grow, and mature in their journey to multiply.

SPIRITUAL CHILDREN

We are called to pass on what the Lord has taught us to a next generation of believers. I am not talking about younger people, but anyone who would be willing to be disciples in the faith, regardless of their age. I have discipled a man who could have been my father. He had been a believer for some time but failed to grow in Christ. Spiritually, he was still a baby. "For though by this time you ought to be teachers, you need someone to teach you again the basic principles of the oracles of God. You need milk, not solid food, for everyone who lives on milk is unskilled in the word of righteousness, since he is a child." (Hebrews 5:12)

Helping another grow in Christ is to teach them the basic principles of the faith. We don't have to be theologians or trained in Bible exposition. We all have experienced how the Word of God has changed our lives and have had encounters with Christ at some level. We are to pass on what we have learned and help them to read the Bible, to pray and apply the Scriptures.

Our first responsibility should be to our own children. They catch, first of all what they see us doing. Our example is the most important.
Then we can look to help younger people. They are often looking for someone older and wiser to mentor them.
Of course, we should remain open to anyone who God brings across our path, with whom God gives us a connection.

God will give you people, as he gave them to Jesus to disciple. "I have manifested your name to the people whom you gave me out of the world. Yours they were, and you gave them to me, and they have kept your word." (John 17:6)

When we sense that the Lord is giving us someone, we need to take the initiative to start a spiritual journey with them. It may just be as simple as having coffee or breakfast together, and asking them; "where are you on your spiritual journey? Could we read the Bible together?" You could do a Bible study together or discuss a book, a chapter a week. Develop the art of asking questions. You don't need to know all the answers, but you can start to discover answers together.
Your goal is not to make followers, but to encourage them to know Christ, grow in Him and make Him known to people around them.
So, how do I get started helping someone become a disciple and be a spiritual mother or father to them?

First, I need to build a relationship.
Biblical truth and godly values are best understood in a the setting of a relationship.
When talking to my children, I learned to appeal to our relationship, which is characterized by love and the desire to help them grow. This is much more effective than talking from a position of authority.
Second, we should be an example to them.

Second, our example is of utmost importance. Godly values are more caught than taught. We live in glass houses and people are

watching us all the time. Our actions and attitudes communicate what we believe in and what we find most important.
Finally, share the truth.

Passing our values on to our children includes instruction. Instilling biblical values requires a commitment to teach our children – consistently, repeatedly, and at every opportunity
– that there is a standard of right and wrong that transcends human opinion.

BORN TO REPRODUCE

 I have been privileged to be around the Navigators movement since my early student days in 1968. The Navigators was founded by Dawson Trotman, who practiced multiplying disciples.
In his classic booklet *Born to Reproduce*,[64] he explains that God has given most people the same basic materials to work with: two hands, two eyes, a nose, a heart, and a couple of hands and legs. What's more, he notes specifically: "Isn't it wonderful that God did not select the wealthy and the educated and say, 'You can have children,' while saying to the poor and the uneducated, 'You cannot'?"
Everyone can reproduce – if not physically, then spiritually. The first order ever given to mankind was: *"Be fruitful and multiply"* (Genesis 1:28). But we see very quickly that God didn't just want lots of warm bodies on the earth. He got that and wiped them away in a flood.
So, if simple numbers weren't what He wanted, what was He after? God answers this question in Malachi 2:15. "Did he not make them one, with a portion of the Spirit in their union? And what was the one God seeking? Godly offspring."

Dawson Trotman writes, "Soul-winners are not soul-winners because of what they know, but because of the Person they know, how well they know Him and how much they long for others to know Him.

"Nothing under Heaven except sin, immaturity and lack of fellowship will put you in a position where you cannot reproduce. Furthermore, there is not anything under Heaven that can keep a newly born-again one from going on with the Lord if he has a spiritual parent to take care of him and give him the spiritual food God has provided for his normal growth."

Effects obey their causes by irresistible laws. When you sow the seed of God's word, you will get results. Not every heart will receive the word, but some will, and the new birth will take place. When a soul is born, give it the care that Paul gave new believers. He believed in follow-up work. He was a busy evangelist, but he took time for follow up. The New Testament consists largely of his follow-up letters to converts.

Dawson Trotman was always asking us, "Where is your man? Where is your woman? Where is your boy? Where is your girl? There are many hearts ready for the gospel now."

You will find God directing you to those whom you can lead to Christ.

THE POWER OF ONE

I met Graham Power at the European Economic Summit a few years ago. I was impressed by what God can do through one person who is fully dedicated to His service. Here is a short description of his story. [65]

Graham started his company in 1983 with its core purpose to "improve the quality of life in Africa through infrastructure development." The Power Group (www.powergrp.co.za) is one of Africa's leading construction firms.

Graham explains how his organization differs from other companies. "The people relationships in Power Group are very special, and love and care for each other is undoubtedly the key to our success." He would say *"not by might, nor by power, but by my Spirit, says the Lord of Hosts"* (Zechariah 4:6).

The company has made its mark in the world of construction, building, and property development. Through pursuing its stated purpose, Graham has built his company into a powerful tool in

God's hands for transformation that is impacting his industry, the nation, and even the world.

The Power Group employs more than 1500 staff members. In 2001, Graham initiated a stadium gathering in Cape Town that saw 45,000 Christians pray for the needs of their nation.
By 2010, this movement grew to become the largest prayer gathering in recorded history as some 350 million people from 220 nations participated in the Global Day of Prayer (GDOP) on Pentecost Sunday. [66]

Graham also founded Unashamedly Ethical, a campaign promoting ethics, values, and clean living through local communities all over the world. [167] Presently active in 143 nations, it challenges individuals and companies to be ethical in all their dealings. The campaign is built upon three pillars around which local communities form: good values, ethics, and clean living. Graham is the first to say that God deserves all the glory and honor for this miraculous work. Truly, the stories of the Global Day of Prayer and Unashamedly Ethical are not the stories of one man's determination; neither are they stories about mighty global organizations; rather, they are a testimony to God's power and grace.

Graham's favorite Scripture is 2 Chronicles 7:14, "If my people who are called by my name humble themselves, and pray and seek my face and turn from their wicked ways, then I will hear from heaven and forgive their sin and heal their land." Graham strongly believes that there will be a dynamic global revival in the near future, following the "waves" of (1) prayer; (2) ethics, values, and clean living; and (3) healing of our land.
Using his business for kingdom purposes, Graham is a generous giver. He builds low-cost housing for the poor, employs people who find it hard to get a job, and looks after his employee-families' health and well-being. He says he is the priest in his company, and the business is his parish. Prayer meetings and Bible studies play a key role in the business.

This is just a very brief story of one man who is impacting Africa for Christ. There are many others!
I wonder who led Graham to Christ. I don't know, but I do know they had no idea what kind of widespread, long-term impact that single conversion would bring.

FROM ONE COMES MORE . . .

 You have probably never heard of Edward Kimball. I hadn't until I read this chain of events. [68]
Kimball was a Sunday school teacher who not only prayed for the hyperactive boys in his class but also sought to win
each one to the Lord personally. Teaching young boys is quite a challenge – like herding cats. But he decided he would be intentional with every last one of them.
A young man named Dwight didn't seem to understand what the gospel was about, so Kimball went to visit him at the shoe store where he stocked shelves. Finding Dwight in the stockroom, he confronted him with the importance of
a personal relationship with Jesus Christ. That young man was Dwight L. Moody. In the stockroom on that Saturday, he believed the gospel and received Jesus Christ as his savior. In his lifetime, Moody touched two continents for God, with thousands professing Christ through his ministry.

But the story doesn't end there. That's only the beginning. Under Moody, another man's heart was touched for God, Wilbur Chapman. Chapman became the evangelist who preached to thousands. One day a professional ball player had a day off and attended one of Chapman's meetings. Billy Sunday said yes to Jesus and walked away from his beloved baseball career to become part of Chapman's team. When Chapman later accepted the pastorate of a large church, Billy Sunday began his own evangelistic crusades.
Another young man, Mordecai Ham, was converted. When Ham came to Charlotte, North Carolina, to preach, a sandy- haired, lanky young man, then in high school, vowed that he wouldn't go

hear Ham preach. But Billy Frank, as he was called by his family, did eventually go.
In May of 1934, Christian businessmen in Charlotte, North Carolina, held an all-day prayer meeting on a pasture owned by Billy Frank's dad. Billy's dad attended, of course, and later recalled one of the men's prayers that day: ". . . that out of Charlotte the Lord would raise up someone to preach the gospel to the ends of the earth." That night Billy Frank went to the preaching service and was intrigued by what he heard. Returning another night, he responded to the invitation and was converted. Billy Frank eventually became known as Billy Graham, the evangelist who preached to more people than any other person who ever lived, including the Apostle Paul!

This fascinating chain of events was triggered by one Sunday school teacher's passion to see his boys know about Jesus. Maybe you've thought about quitting because you didn't think you were making any difference. Next time you are tempted to give up, remember Edward Kimball, whose persistence and faithfulness were tremendously honored by the Lord. The story would be very different if Edward Kimball had not visited young Dwight Moody on a Saturday in a shoe store.
You never know how many seeds will come out of one apple! The Lord can easily multiply the harvest.

DAY 29: QUESTIONS TO PONDER

Do you believe that one person whom you could help on their discipleship journey has the potential to help others?

Who is God giving you "out of the world" with whom you can build a relationship, share your life, build them up and send them out?

Describe God's part and my part in developing "spiritual children."

DAY 30: FINISHING WELL

KEY VERSE

"I glorified you on earth, having accomplished the work that you gave me to do."

John 17:4

J esus was leaving the disciples after more than three years together. Peter didn't want their friendship to end. Was his friend and leader leaving?

Jesus didn't appear eager to leave, After dying and rising from the grave, He lingered forty more days with His friends before going to be with the Father. But Jesus had to leave so that Peter and friends could carry on the ministry. *"Nevertheless, I tell you the truth: it is to your advantage that I go away, for if I do not go away, the Helper will not come to you. But if I go, I will send him to you"* (John 16:7).

Jesus laid the foundation, and the apostles carried on the work that they were trained and equipped to do.

Now was the time to pass the baton to others to carry on the race! When Moses finished his task, and had laid a good foundation, he passed the baton to Joshua, who took God's assignment further. Moses' task was to take the people out of Egypt, Joshua's task was to get the people into the land promised to them.

Moses received the original command but Joshua was chosen to bring it to completion.

It is sobering to realise that such a spiritual warrior as Joshua was unable to pass on the baton himself. The Bible says that after Joshua and his generation died, another generation grew up that did not acknowledge the Lord. Joshua received the baton but failed to pass it on!

The well-known speaker, Dr. Myles Munro, passed away in a plane crash in 2014. Shortly before he died, he told of a dream in which he saw an athlete lying in a coffin clutching a baton.

The dream was a vision of failure, someone hanging onto a baton instead of passing it on. Batons exist to be passed, not kept. [69]

I am very thankful for men like Larry Burkett and Howard Dayton, pioneers of biblical financial teaching; they knew how to pass the baton. They envisioned, built, and passed on to qualified disciples the mission to learn, apply, and multiply biblical financial principles. All so that people may know Christ more intimately, be free to serve Him, and carry out the Great Commission.

I am thankful for men in The Navigators who mentored and discipled me for many years, imparting to me an urgency and a way to "know Christ and to make Him known."

However, I have also known ministry leaders and business leaders who failed to do that. I have observed that it is very difficult for pioneers in business and ministry to open their hands and complete their stewardship by passing the baton to the next generation.

Juan Carlos Ortiz tells the story of meeting an old lady in his native Argentina who introduced him to one of her great-granddaughters. She went on to tell that she had six children and thirty-six grandchildren. Her family was impressive in number, and among her grandchildren were many well-educated and professional people.

Carlos asked her, "How did you manage to produce such a large, well-fed, well-dressed, well-educated, extended family?"

She replied, "I didn't. I just took care of the six. And each of them took care of their six." [70]

ELIJAH AND ELISHA

Elijah has just experienced the mighty power of God on Mount Carmel as the Baal priests were defeated in an amazing

pyrotechnic display. Now, he was depressed, hiding in a cave on another mountain, fearing for his life.
God asked him, "What are you doing here, Elijah?" Elijah replied, "He said, "I have been very jealous for the LORD, the God of hosts. For the people of Israel have forsaken your covenant, thrown down your altars, and killed your prophets with the sword, and I, even I only, am left, and they seek my life, to take it away." (1 Kings 19:13, 14. He felt he was on his own, in danger of his life and that there was no one else to carry on his work.

In fact, there were 7,000 faithful ones who had not succumbed to Baal. He was not really alone.
Elijah needed to recognize that the Lord had already solved the problem. Elijah had to go and pass on the baton! "The Lord said to him, ""Go, return on your way to the wilderness of Damascus … Elisha the son of Shaphat of Abel-meholah you shall anoint to be prophet in your place." (1 Kings 19:15,16)
Elijah looked in the right place (see 1 Kings 19:19).

There are two notable points about passing on the baton, which we read in 1 Kings 19:19.
First, Elijah found Elisha 'in the field.' When looking for the one God has chosen for us to pass on the baton, look for those who are already working 'in the field.' They are those faithful ones who already have the willingness to work and the vision for the work.

Second, Elijah passed on to Elisha a visible, tangible sign of God-given authority. He gave Elisha his mantle, symbolizing prophetic authority, which he received when ordained and set apart for a special task. Later, we read (2 Kings 2:13,14) that Elisha took that same mantle and opened the river Jordan for them to cross.

HOW DID ELISHA EXPERIENCE THIS CHANGE IN LEADERSHIP?

Elisha was willing for follow Elijah and recognized God's call on his life. He started out by burning his bridges. He sacrificed his means of livelihood, his oxen and yokes, and laid on a feast, thereby publicly announcing new ministry.

Elisha lived with Elijah for some time. Elisha continued to learn from Elijah as they served the Lord together. After Elijah was called up into heaven, with 'chariots of fire' the passing of the baton was finished, and the other prophets declared, "The spirit of Elijah rests on Elisha." (2 Kings 2:15)

Elisha persevered, even when Elijah wanted to say "Go away!" (2 Kings 2:1-8). Regardless of Elijah's response, Elisha demonstrated tenacity and commitment. Elisha was not going to let go. It is this perseverance that develops a commitment to finish the race, whatever it takes.
Elisha emulated Elijah because they lived life together (2 Kings 2:9-25).
After Elijah ascended into heaven and the passing of the baton was complete, the people of Jericho immediately recognized that *"The spirit of Elijah rests on Elisha"* (verse 15). In other words, Elisha was running the same race Elijah had been running with the same purpose and in the same way.
To successfully pass the baton from one to another, we must live life together, running at the same pace with the same cadence and purpose so when it is time to complete the pass, there will be no stumble, hesitation, or drop.

PAUL AND TIMOTHY

Paul recognized he had a responsibility to train up others. He found ". . . Timothy, the son of a Jewish woman who was a believer, but his father was a Greek. He was well spoken of by the brothers at Lystra and Iconium" (Acts 16:1-2). Paul, wanting Timothy to accompany him in ministry, discipled, trained, and taught him. They are a great example of what we all should be doing. Find a Paul from whom you can learn and a Timothy to whom you can pass it on.
Paul described their close friendship: "But you know Timothy's proven worth, how as a son with a father he has served with me in the gospel" (Philippians 2:22). He could confidently send Timothy

to teach others. "That is why I sent you Timothy, my beloved and faithful child in the Lord, to remind you of my ways in Christ, as I teach them everywhere in every church" (1 Corinthians 4:17).

Paul and Timothy travelled extensively together, experiencing a lot, including imprisonment. Timothy had lots of opportunity to observe Paul's life, and listen to his teaching.
Timothy showed himself faithful, so Paul trusted him enough to send him on mission on his own to remind the brethren of his teachings.
In Acts 16, we read about Paul and Timothy on mission together. After Timothy joined Paul, they got down to work straight away. They travelled through the cities, strengthening the churches and seeing many come to faith. They communicated important decisions which had been made in Jerusalem to the churches. Timothy learned about the importance of being led by the Holy Spirit. When they wanted to go into Asia, 'the Spirit of Jesus did not allow them.' (verse 7) They were led to go in a different direction, towards Macedonia. Paul received a special vision from the Lord, starting a ministry in Europe. "And a vision appeared to Paul in the night: a man of Macedonia was standing there, urging him and saying, "Come over to Macedonia and help us." And when Paul had seen the vision, immediately we sought to go on into Macedonia, concluding that God had called us to preach the gospel to them." (verses 9,10)
God then led Timothy and Paul in a new direction. "During the night Paul had a vision of a man of Macedonia standing and begging him, 'Come over to Macedonia and help us'" (verse 9).

Not surprisingly, Paul took this as clear guidance that God had indeed called them to go into Europe and preach the gospel to the people in Philippi. (Acts 16:10).
There, Timothy and Paul met a group of women down by the river at a place of prayer (verse 13). They told them about Jesus and, Lydia, a rich merchant, was converted. She invited Paul and Timothy to her home and stay with her household. It must have been an extraordinary and wonderful experience for them both to

see how the "Lord opened her heart to respond to Paul's message" (verse 14).

Together, they experienced how "the Lord opened her heart to pay attention to what was said by Paul." (verse 14)The final letter attributed to Paul is 2 Timothy, written from Rome around 67 A.D. Speaking about the dangers of false teachers, Paul wrote to Timothy, "You, however, have followed my teaching, my conduct, my aim in life, my faith, my patience, my love, my steadfastness, my persecutions and sufferings…" (2 Timothy 3:10-11). Timothy had seen Paul, followed him, and carried on his work.
Paul's priority was encouraging and empowering the next generation, right to the end of his days. Let's make it ours too!

FINISHING WELL

 When praying for His disciples in the Garden of Gethsemane, Jesus said to the Father, "I glorified you on earth, having accomplished the work that you gave me to do" (John 17:4). This was before accomplishing His work of redemption on the cross: this referred to the work of training the disciples.

When people used to ask evangelist Billy Graham how they could pray for him, he invariably responded, "Pray that I finish my life well and don't dishonor the Lord." He recognized how rare it is for people to remain faithful to the Lord, fully engaged in their calling to the end.
According to Dr. Howard Hendricks, of the 2,930 individuals mentioned in the Bible, we know significant details about only 100 of them. Of those 100, only about one-third finished well. Of the two-thirds that did not finish well, most failed in the second half of their lives.

Finishing well for those who are wealthy is especially challenging because of the options money can buy. Many of these can distract us from serving Christ. A friend recently heard a pastor teach that people will often say "I either need more money or I need God to

come through." The problem with that is we think money is the solution to our problems. I
believe wealthy people often go immediately to their money to solve problems, not giving much thought to God's solutions. Money is rarely a complete solution – even to financial problems. It can alleviate symptoms, but the root goes deeper. Because the root is typically a spiritual, relational, psychological, or moral issue, so are the solutions. If those of us who are rich don't feel the need to ask God for much, we are not developing an intimate relationship with Him. And we may be missing many of His valuable life lessons.
In your journey with the Lord, it's not how you start that matters; it's how you finish. What are you doing to become the one in three who reaches the finish line still serving Christ?
You will need spiritual discipline to have a strong finishing kick when you hit the tape at age 65, 75, 85, or whatever age God calls you home.

It is your ability to persevere through life's challenges and endure throughout tough times which will determine if you can finish well. Endurance is the by-product of godly character. As Scripture says, *"Therefore, since we have so great a cloud of witnesses surrounding us, let us also lay aside every encumbrance and the sin which so easily entangles us, and let us run with endurance the race that is set before us, fixing our eyes on Jesus . . ."* (Hebrews 12:1-2, NASB1995).
Finishing well does not mean finishing with a perfect record. But it does mean learning from our mistakes, getting back on course, and pursuing Christ with our whole heart. We are to work hard in building the kingdom of God as long as we are able, despite any previous mistakes we may have made. As you read these words, you may think it's already too late for you to finish well. Perhaps you've made some big boneheaded mistakes. Many of those who finished well in the Bible were guilty of terrible decisions. Abraham lied. Moses committed murder. David was an adulterer and a murderer. Peter denied Christ three times.

The Christian life isn't a hundred-yard sprint but more like a marathon. Distance racing requires grit, determination, and finishing power – not speed.

Paul, the murderous persecutor of the early church, said it this way: ". . . But one thing I do: forgetting what lies behind and straining forward to what lies ahead, I press on toward the goal for the prize of the upward call of God in Christ Jesus" (Philippians 3:13-14).

Aging is an inevitable part of life. Although it imposes certain limitations, we need to embrace God's perspective. As John Quincy Adams was nearing the end of his life, a friend asked how he was doing. "John Quincy Adams is well, quite well," replied the sixth president of the United States. "But the house in which he lives at present is becoming quite dilapidated.

It's tottering upon its foundations. Time has nearly destroyed it. Its roof is pretty well worn out. It is becoming almost uninhabitable, and I think John Quincy Adams will have to move out of it soon. But he himself is quite well, quite well." [11]

The apostle Paul tells us, "For we know that if the earthly tent which is our house is torn down, we have a building from God, a house not made with hands, eternal in the heavens. For indeed in this house we groan, longing to be clothed with our dwelling from heaven" (2 Corinthians 5:1-2).

As we age, we are encouraged to concentrate on developing a closer relationship with the Lord. "Therefore we do not lose heart, but though our outer man is decaying, yet our inner man is being renewed day by day" (2 Corinthians 4:16).

Albert Diepeveen has mentored me for almost three decades. Albert and his wife, Theresa, are in their late eighties. They are more in love with Christ and with each other than ever before. They continue to invest in the lives of others in their church, city, and around the world. The Psalmist wrote, "The righteous will flourish like a palm tree . . . They will still bear fruit in old age, they will stay fresh and green" (Psalm 92:12, 14, NIV).

Think of all those who have led enormously productive lives in old age. While in their eighties, Moses led the children of Israel out of captivity. Winston Churchill wrote his four-volume *A History of the English-Speaking Peoples.* "Colonel" Harland Sanders founded the Kentucky Fried Chicken (KFC) restaurant chain. Mother Teresa tirelessly served Calcutta's poor.

Here are some of the most common reasons that wealthy followers of Christ do not finish well.

1. Distorted (unbiblical) view of retirement and leisure

2. Not fulfilling God's calling

3. Debt

4. Dishonesty

5. Marital dysfunction

6. Not seeking counsel or having accountable relationships

7. Not growing in their relationship with Christ

8. Not using wealth to multiply God's kingdom.

I believe most of us will not finish well without the encouragement and accountability of someone else. It is essential to nurture a relationship with a small group or at least one or two people with whom you have built a friendship based on trust, confidentiality, and accountability. In other words, friends who are close enough and love you enough to confront you if need be.

Here are several suggestions that will help you identify a small group or friend with whom you can become accountable.

1. Pray for the Lord to bring just the right person or people into your life.

2. Limit your search to those who you sense are sincere about growing closer to Christ.
3. Seek those whose company you genuinely enjoy.
4. Do not choose people that you will not be able to trust with confidentiality.

When you look back on your life, I am confident that the greatest joy you can have is seeing your children and your spiritual children be faithful to Christ. At the end of the first century, the Apostle John wrote, *"I have no greater joy than to hear that my children are walking in the truth"* (3 John 1:4, NIV).

Just imagine getting to heaven and meeting all those people we were able to help on their journey with Jesus. "Well done, good and faithful servant. You have been faithful with little; I will set you over much. Enter into the joy of your master" (Matthew 25:21). That is finishing well!

IN CLOSING

Thank you for spending this time with us. In closing, I'd like to leave you with a few thoughts that have been powerful motivators for me.

Nothing on this planet comes close to knowing Jesus Christ and living a life that pleases Him.

Jesus finished well when He said, "I glorified you on earth, having accomplished the work that you gave me to do" (John 17:4).

Paul finished well when he said, *"I have fought the good fight, I have finished the course, I have kept the faith"* (2 Timothy 4:7, NASB).

I am not ready to retire just yet. The call of Jesus is still strong, but I do want to finish strong, in the whole armor of God, obeying His commands, and seeing the enemy defeated and friends entering the kingdom.

My prayer is that you will finish well, too. That you will complete the task the Lord has given you so that you will hear these words ring in your ears throughout eternity: *"Well done, good and faithful servant . . . enter into the joy of your master"* (Matthew 25:21).

DAY 29: QUESTIONS TO PONDER

297

What does finishing well look like as a financial disciple?

What are you doing in your effort to finish well?

Who can help you and hold you accountable on your finishing well journey?

DAY 29: QUESTIONS TO PONDER

About Compass

Compass - finances God's way is a global, non-denominational movement teaching financial discipleship and generosity.

The purpose is to serve churches, businesses, ministries, schools and other organizations by providing biblically based solutions on handling money and possessions.
Compass' mission is to help people everywhere to learn, apply and teach Gods financial and business principles. We are looking for three major outcomes.

1. To know Christ more intimately as we trust and obey Him, experiencing Christ at work.

2. To become free from worry, fear, stress and anxiety and then be free to serve and love the Lord and our neighbors.

3. To contribute to fulfilling the Great Commission by passing on what we have learned to others and making 'financial disciples.'

Compass has developed a wide range of resources in a wide variety of formats, such as workshops, small group studies, e-books and online learning.

There are teaching resources for all ages, from small children through students to adults; with application to areas of life such as business, church, marriage and family.

To see our resources, please visit the web site at
www.compass1.eu

References

1 https://www.franklincovey-benelux.com/en/tips-tools/habit-2-begin-with-the-end-in-mind/

2 Alice in Wonderland by Lewis Carroll. Simon and Schuster 2019

3 https://accountable2you.com/blog/accountable-to-god/

4 https://generositymonk.com/meditations/page/374/

5 https://dtbm.org/ownership/

6 Erwin W. Lutzer, "Your Eternal Reward, Triumph and Tease at the Judgement Seat of Christ," 2015, Moody Publishers.

7 http://www.biblestudymanuals.net/your_eternal_reward.htm

8 http://www.rayfowler.org/sermons/real-answers-about-heaven/judgment-and-eternal-rewards/

9 Surprised by Hope: Rethinking Heaven, the Resurrection, and the Mission of the Church, by N.T. Wright. 2009, published by Harper One.

10 https://en.wikiquote.org/wiki/Talk:Augustine_of_Hippo

11 http://lifeinjesus-ministries.com/JSEAT1.html

12 https://ccel.org/ccel/melanchthon/apology/apology.ix.html

13 Spurgeon, "Justification and Glory," MTP, 11:249

14 https://www.church-of-yehovah.org/rulecity.html

15 https://www.blueletterbible.org/devotionals/me/view.cfm?Date=05/14&Time=both&body=1

16 Quoted by Erwin Lutzer in https://www.biblestudymanuals.net/your_eternal_reward.htm

17 https://www.vcyamerica.org/redeeming-the-time/2020/12/01/tozers-four-questions/

18 https://kinginstitute.stanford.edu/king-papers/publications/autobiography-martin-luther-king-jr-contents/chapter-4-boston-university

19 https://www.epm.org/blog/2014/Dec/17/live-line

[20] https://revpacman.com/2017/07/17/the-70-resolutions-of-jonathan-edwards/

[21] https://anglicanconnection.com/living-in-the-light-of-eternity-in-a-troubled-world/

[22] Quoted in https://www.desiringgod.org/articles/this-day-and-that-day

[23] https://deeperchristianquotes.com/what-is-its-eternity-value-john-wesley/

[24] C.S. Lewis, "The Screwtape Letters", 1942. William Collins Sons & Co.

[25] https://www.desiringgod.org/articles/the-resolutions-of-jonathan-edwards

[26] https://www.biblestudymanuals.net/your_eternal_reward.htm

[27] https://en.wikipedia.org/wiki/Charles_Studd

[28] https://renewaljournal.com/2017/11/29/the-true-story-behind-the-song-i-have-decided-to-follow-jesus/

[29] https://en.wikipedia.org/wiki/When_I_Survey_the_Wondrous_Cross

[30] Lectures on Revival" by Charles G. Finney. Bethany House Publishers. 92

[31] https://utmost.org/classic/after-surrender-what-classic/2/

[32] https://moodycenter.org/the-quotable-moody-d-l-moody-quotes/

[33] Told by Ravi Zacharias in "can a Man Live Without God?" p199. 1994. Word Books.

[34] https://www.theopedia.com/joy

[35] https://www.mentalhealthtoday.co.uk/people-were-happier-in-1957-than-today-according-to-research

[36] Translated by author from "Auswege aus dem Streben nach immer mehr," by Anselm Grün. Vier-Türme GmbH, Verlag, Münsterschwarzach, 2015

[37] https://edcchristian.com/2018/02/02/the-allowances-of-the-heart/

38 https://en.wikipedia.org/wiki/
Stanford_marshmallow_experiment

39 http://love-mediagenr.blogspot.com/2016/03/masters-of-
love.html

40 https://www.journeyofhearts.org/kirstimd/friendship.htm

41 https://bible.org/illustration/house-dying

42 https://sermons.faithlife.com/sermons/724753-walking-with-
gentleness

43 Edmund Burke "Letter to a Member of the National Assembly,"
1791.—The Works of the Right Honorable Edmund Burke, vol. 4, pp.
51–52 (1899).

44 Economics of Good and Evil by Tomas Sedlacek. Oxford
University Press; Illustrated edition (2013)

45 https://seths.blog/2012/04/if-your-happiness-is-based-on-
always-getting-a-little-more-than-youve-got/

46 https://www.lifeway.com/en/articles/sermon-avoid-pitfalls-
riches-money-greed-1-timothy-6

47 http://storage.cloversites.com/crossbridgechurch/documents/
Simplicity.pdf

48 https://www.dailymail.co.uk/news/article-1227867/
The-33-000-year-Oxford-don-giving-1m-African-aid.html

49 https://www.givingwhatwecan.org

50 Richard Swenson, M.D. "Margin: Restoring Emotional, Physical
and Time Reserves to Overloaded Lives." 2004, Navpress

51 https://bible.org/illustration/prime-pump

52 Walter Bruegemann in The Other Side, November-December
2001, Vol. 37, No. 5.

53 *God and Money: How We Discovered True Riches at Harvard
Business School,* authors Gregory Baumer and John Cortines .
2016. Rose Publishing

54 https://moodycenter.org/the-quotable-moody-d-l-moody-
quotes/

55 Schindler's List, 1993 directed and produced by Steven
Spielberg and written by Steven Zaillian.

56 https://www.barrypopik.com/index.php/new_york_city/entry/show_me_your_checkbook_and_ill_tell_you_your_values

57 https://www.famousquotes123.com/billy-graham-quotes.html

58 https://bible.org/seriespage/lesson-21-prescription-contentment-1-timothy-66-8

59 https://hymnary.org/text/on_a_hill_far_away_stood_an_old_rugged

60 C.S. Lewis, "Letters to an American Lady." 2014. Wm. B. Eerdmans Publishing Co

61 https://hymnary.org/text/take_my_life_and_let_it_be

62 Journal excerpt from Shadow of the Almighty (1989) by Elisabeth Elliot, Jim Elliot, 1949

63 The Master Plan of Evangelism, by Robert E. Coleman. 1972 Fleming H. Revell Company

64 Born to Reproduce, by Dawson Trotman, 1970, Back to the Bible Broadcast.

65 https://www.entrepreneurialleaders.com/2012-GrahamPower

66 https://www.globalvoiceofprayer.com/about-us/

67 www.unashamedlyethical.com

68 http://www.travisagnew.org/2013/07/22/the-chain-of-events-for-billy-grahams-conversion/   and https://billygraham.org/story/the-night-billy-graham-was-born-again/

69 Told by Nicky Gumbel in https://www.premiernexgen.com/premier-ycw-magazine/nicky-gumbel-three-ways-to-empower-the-next-generation/9300.article

70 Quoted from https://www.gty.org/library/Print/Blog/B160926